Cambridge Elements

Elements in the History of Philosophy and Theology in the West
edited by
Alexander J. B. Hampton
University of Toronto

A CRITICAL GENEALOGY OF HUMANISM

Friedemann Stengel
Martin Luther University Halle-Wittenberg

Shaftesbury Road, Cambridge CB2 8EA, United Kingdom

One Liberty Plaza, 20th Floor, New York, NY 10006, USA

477 Williamstown Road, Port Melbourne, VIC 3207, Australia

314–321, 3rd Floor, Plot 3, Splendor Forum, Jasola District Centre,
New Delhi – 110025, India

Cambridge University Press is part of Cambridge University Press & Assessment,
a department of the University of Cambridge.

We share the University's mission to contribute to society through the pursuit of
education, learning and research at the highest international levels of excellence.

www.cambridge.org
Information on this title: www.cambridge.org/9781009634267

DOI: 10.1017/9781009634236

© Friedemann Stengel 2026

This publication is in copyright. Subject to statutory exception and to the provisions
of relevant collective licensing agreements, with the exception of the Creative
Commons version the link for which is provided below, no reproduction of any
part may take place without the written permission of Cambridge University
Press & Assessment.

An online version of this work is published at doi.org/10.1017/9781009634236 under
a Creative Commons Open Access license CC-BY-NC 4.0 which permits re-use,
distribution and reproduction in any medium for non-commercial purposes providing
appropriate credit to the original work is given and any changes made are indicated.
To view a copy of this license visit https://creativecommons.org/licenses/by-nc/4.0

When citing this work, please include a reference to the DOI 10.1017/9781009634236

First published 2026

A catalogue record for this publication is available from the British Library

ISBN 978-1-009-63426-7 Hardback
ISBN 978-1-009-63424-3 Paperback
ISSN 3033-3954 (online)
ISSN 3033-3946 (print)

Cambridge University Press & Assessment has no responsibility for the persistence or
accuracy of URLs for external or third-party internet websites referred to in this
publication and does not guarantee that any content on such websites is, or will
remain, accurate or appropriate.

For EU product safety concerns, contact us at Calle de José Abascal, 56, 1°, 28003
Madrid, Spain, or email eugpsr@cambridge.org

A Critical Genealogy of Humanism

Elements in the History of Philosophy and Theology
in the West

DOI: 10.1017/9781009634236
First published online: January 2026

Friedemann Stengel
Martin Luther University Halle-Wittenberg

Author for correspondence: Friedemann Stengel,
friedemann.stengel@theologie.uni-halle.de

Abstract: "Humanism" is among the most powerful terms in historical and contemporary political, religious, and philosophical debates. The term serves to position itself in ideological conflicts and to cement a claim to interpretation, but is highly contradictory. This Element addresses "humanism" in its striking contradictions. Contemporary definitions are confronted with the historical contexts the term "humanism" is applied to. Based on Niethammer's invention of "humanism" as an anti-Enlightenment pedagogical concept (1808), the book does not present a mere conceptual history but rather a theoretically oriented discourse, an examination of the opposing positions, between which humanism has been constructed. In this way, its "impossibility" is shown, which is rooted in its strict contextuality. Secondly, historiographical alternatives to this dilemma are pointed out, in order to finally give suggestions not only for an ethical-normative work of the historian of humanism but for dealing with "humanism" in general, in connection with discourse-theoretical suggestions. This title is also available as open access on Cambridge Core.

Keywords: humanism, discourse theory, historiography, socialism, 19th century

© Friedemann Stengel 2026

ISBNs: 9781009634267 (HB), 9781009634243 (PB), 9781009634236 (OC)
ISSNs: 3033-3954 (online), 3033-3946 (print)

Contents

1 On the Impossibility of a Concept: Early and Late Aporias in Humanism   1

2 "Humanism" in the 19th Century: Between Education, Religion, and History   13

3 Ways out of the Humanism Dilemma   38

    References   55

1 On the Impossibility of a Concept: Early and Late Aporias in Humanism

1.1 A Lexical Entry

The term "humanism" appears in academic and media debates across the globe in a variety of languages and cultures. But the inconsistent, polemical, and conflicting ways in which humanism has been defined throughout history persist. Adding to these challenges are the unresolvable disparities between various definitions of humanisms as they pertain to the Renaissance, the Christian humanisms of the 19th and 20th centuries, the SED's Marxist-Leninist religious policy directed against the churches,[1] which sought to legitimize the categories of reconciliation or struggle,[2] or some more recent humanistic associations that portray humanism as an anti-Christian or an exclusively anti-religious worldview.[3] Additionally, the official Russian position, represented by Vladimir Putin, and the official Russian Orthodox position, represented by Patriarch Kirill I, further views humanism as a Western, liberal, heretical ideology linked to homosexuality, capitalism, and anti-Russian tendencies, which must be fought both politically and militarily at all costs.[4]

A recent article on humanism in a sixteen-volume German encyclopedia on early modern history, *Enzyklopädie der Neuzeit* (Encyclopedia of Early Modern History, hereinafter *Enzyklopädie*), both thematizes and reproduces the problem of a highly divergent and contradictory understanding of humanism. Presenting "humanism" in all its compelling, multifaceted dimensions as a notion that is historically, culturally, and anthropologically charged, it rejects its "ideological" association with the Renaissance. However, strangely contradicting a claim made at the beginning of the article to the effect that humanism represents the "most important and most effective European educational movement" of the modern era before the Enlightenment,[5] it supports the notion that humanism began to designate an epoch, specifically the 15th and 16th centuries, as a matter of course, starting in the second half of the 19th century. The *Enzyklopädie* article asserts that humanism was not a clearly defined phenomenon in the 15th and 16th centuries, neither conceptually nor in terms of content, and adds that the sole point of reference in the Renaissance and the Reformation was *studia humanitatis*, the foundation of *artes liberales*, or the liberal arts, whereby the term *humanista* was a collective term denoting those who taught

---

[1] The ecclesiastical genesis of the concept of humanism in the GDR needs more careful study. Cf. meanwhile Baab, 2013: 129–32; Stengel, 2013a: 357–8.
[2] Cf. Blume, 2021. On the ambivalent interpretation of humanism by the SED and the CDU in the GDR and its reception in African contexts cf. Blume, 2022.
[3] Cf. Baab, 2013: 133–47 passim; Fincke, 2002; Fincke, 2004.
[4] Cf. for the time Tomyuk, 2023; Tomyuk, 2022.
[5] Cf. Walther, 2007a: 665–6.

and studied the corresponding branches of learning.[6] The contention is that it is improbable for that strand of humanism to have had consistent anthropological implications resembling the humanism first conceived in the early 19th century.[7] Described elsewhere is another paradox, namely that humanism, as a historically acknowledged epochal designation, is endowed with a certain "normative authority" despite the fact that in the 15th and 16th centuries, humanism signified neither humanity nor individuality, as it was commonly believed in the 19th century, nor did it aim to propagate tolerance as the Enlightenment overtly did later.[8] Last but not least, it claims that humanism increasingly collided with confessionalism even as it continued to be seen as a "supporting pillar" of European education until the end of the 20th century.[9]

Is humanism a spirit or an entity whose "spiritual vitality" is not rooted in faith but rather in a larger worldly context and "elegantly"[10] ignored the churches? Is humanism affiliated with Christianity, or is it a rival system? Is it an era when the Middle Ages transitioned to the so-called early modern era, thus representing the key "indicator of an epochal change – in Western mentality, culture and civilization"?[11] At least that is what the article in *Enzyklopädie* claims. But one would need to add to that another question: Is humanism merely anthropological or is it a pedagogical concept that emerged in the context of a specific Enlightenment critique, which devolved into an anti-clerical alternative religion – first in the left Hegelianism of the 19th century and then again in the GDR?

Other articles and definitions in *Enzyklopädie* emphasize the historicity of the notion of humanism to varying degrees: some articles and definitions emphasize the parallels between humanism and Christianity, while others emphasize the differences. However, all treat humanism as both a historical and suprahistorical scholarly concept.[12] The *Enzyklopädie* article recommends using humanism as "an indispensable heuristic tool," which does not directly address the ambiguities and contradictions it also clearly highlights.[13]

How humanism is accounted for in the *Enzyklopädie* article is indeed complicated by the concept of humanism that emerged – amid some controversy – only starting in the 19th century. That is most likely due to the fact that historical concepts were ascribed specific conceptions of the history of

---

[6] Cf. Walther, 2007a: 667–8.
[7] Cf. Walther, 2007a: 668.
[8] Walther, 2007a: 666, 668.
[9] Walther, 2007a: 666.
[10] Walther, 2007a: 675.
[11] Walther, 2007a: 691.
[12] The influential account of the Romance scholar, August Buck, who regards humanism as an educational movement extending from antiquity to the 20th century, is paradigmatic: Cf. Buck, 1987: 9–10.
[13] Walther, 2007a: 668.

ideas, in this instance, dating to the 19th century, even though all of these constructs had been spawned, without exception, in different historical contexts, earlier or later. This raises the question of whether a historical concept, and consequently a historicizing concept, such as humanism, can at all be useful for designating a superhistorical phenomenon.

In what follows, this question will be taken up in relation to the first time that humanism is mentioned as a concept, which even recent studies have dated to the 19th century. The notion that humanism unequivocally came to truly signify a concept starting only in the 19th century is commonly accepted among contemporaries, and almost without exception, also referenced in encyclopedias across the globe. This concept of humanism will be analyzed here according to the criteria set out in the humanism article in *Enzyklopädie*, to compare it with contemporary understandings of humanism. The question of whether a genealogy of humanism can be conceptualized to allow for a more historically consistent definition of humanism – notwithstanding the transformations in the concept of humanism in the 19th century – will be consequently explored in Section 3.4.

1.2 Genealogical Methodology

This investigation adopts a genealogical framework[14] as its methodological foundation – a framework that transcends conventional historiographical perspectives to constitute a rigorous analytical apparatus for interrogating categorical contingency. Within this theoretical architecture, contingency assumes a technical definition distinct from colloquial notions of "chance" or "arbitrariness"; rather, it designates the absence of necessity, wherein necessity itself emerges as a retrospective construction deployed to legitimize contemporary epistemic positions.

As Bergunder eloquently observes, this methodological orientation does not diminish "the power and normative force of hegemonic general concepts"[15] but rather historicizes such power, situating its claims to universality within the particular intellectual battlegrounds from which they emerged. The deployment of Foucaultian "historical ontology" thus becomes not merely an analytical tool but a philosophical stance that eschews the totalizing ambitions of grand ideological projects,[16] subjecting even those ontologies that assert universal significance to contextual scrutiny.

Universal concepts ostensibly maintain stable connections to what may be termed a "transcendental signified" – an entity presumed to transcend historical particularity and maintain invariance across spatiotemporal coordinates.

---

[14] Cf. Bergunder, 2024: 2–8.
[15] Bergunder, 2024: 4.
[16] Foucault, 1990: 49.

However, empirical analysis reveals that such signifiers remain embedded within spatiotemporal matrices, deriving their semantic content and epistemic significance from these very contexts. The absence of genuine transcendence becomes methodologically significant: while these signifiers assert transcendental status, they cannot exist independently of systems of differences,[17] which constitute linguistically and historically meaning through relational positioning rather than absolute reference.

The genealogical approach thus resolves the fundamental tension between categorical abstractions and the material specificity of their emergence. It illuminates how universal categories perpetually conceal their own contextuality – their irreducible particularity – precisely because they crystallize within concrete intellectual confrontations that confer their distinctive semantic signatures. The mere invocation of these categories fails to preserve their originary contexts. Such citation transcends simple repetition to become what Derrida conceptualizes as "iterability"[18] – a process fundamentally distinct from quotation's illusory preservation of original meaning.

Through iteration, original contexts persist only as traces or effects of initial semantic configurations, yet undergo systematic transformation within new contextual frameworks.[19] This mechanism ensures that origins remain recognizable solely as effects; original meanings undergo continuous regeneration within each present moment. Following Žižek's analytical framework, semantic effects operate retroactively: the signifying chain's meaning achieves fixation through present-moment "quilting" that sutures signified to signifier, thereby arresting the perpetual sliding of meanings across the differential network.[20]

Genealogy thus reveals the impossibility of such categories claiming eternity or universality across spatiotemporal dimensions. It transcends traditional conceptual histories that ultimately retain commitment to universal invariant essences, instead pursuing a more sophisticated archaeological project: tracing the specific contexts wherein universality claims emerge – contexts that simultaneously enable and constrain such assertions.

Our research project – dedicated to tracing humanism's conceptual trajectory – employs Foucault's genealogical understanding as its primary methodological instrument. This approach fundamentally rejects mythologies of singular origin for concepts or categories, seeking instead to dispel what Foucault terms "chimeras of the origin."[21] As Bergunder precisely formulates: "In this way,

---

[17] Cf. Derrida, 1972: 424; Derrida, 1986: 56–7, 76.
[18] Derrida, 2001.
[19] Derrida, 2004: 89–90.
[20] Žižek, 1989: 113.
[21] Foucault, 1996: 73; Derrida, 2004: 86, 89.

genealogy serves as a method to critically examine the pre-history of the present, moving step by step from the present into the past."[22]

Our genealogical analysis commences with the recognition that contemporary deployments of "humanism" demonstrate remarkable efficacy yet remain far from uniform; rather, they exhibit profound diversity marked by universal claims that persistently invoke originary meanings, most frequently situated within early modern European or late medieval contexts. From this present vantage point, we interrogate the term's inaugural emergence before exploring the diverse contexts wherein it has been constructed into a universal and potent conceptual apparatus.

1.3 The Invention of Humanism: Niethammer

Friedrich Immanuel Niethammer was upheld as the inventor and architect of the first concept of *humanism* beyond the peripheries of the German-speaking world.[23] His work, entitled *Streit des Philanthropinismus und Humanismus in der Theorie des Erziehungs-Unterrichts unsrer Zeit* (The Dispute between Philanthropinism and Humanism in the Theory of Educational Instruction in our Time) (1808), was well-received across many disciplines in the 19th century, not only pedagogy.[24] Even the title portrays humanism as a contentious pedagogical program.

Niethammer's term "Philanthropinism," instead of Philanthropism, is derived from the reform pedagogical school "Philanthropinum" in Dessau (1774–1793).[25] Niethammer's spelling is used in this Element to avoid confusion with the more general term "philanthropism." But it is crucial to note that the first place where "humanism" is conceived is in a debate about an enlightened educational project. Niethammer's starting point is his very specific, one-sided understanding of Enlightenment pedagogy, against which he drafts "humanism" as a modern counter-program, but which should not be hastily equated with the humanities grammar schools (gymnasiums) that are particularly widespread in German-speaking countries and beyond. Pedagogy is the

---

[22] Bergunder, 2024: 5.
[23] Niethammer, 1808. Given that this is a special literary genre, it is difficult to trace the term back to 1798 in Friedrich Abegg's travel diary. Cf. Wolf, 2004: 549.
[24] In addition to a singular mention of "humanism" in Goethe (1811–14), in connection with morality and religion as a "highly humane" practice in the judiciary, whose reference (perhaps Zedler, see below note 87) does not emerge from the text, there is the direct reference to Niethammer's description of the highly absurd dispute between humanism and philanthropinism, albeit without naming Niethammer, in the work of the educator Herbart (1824–5): vol. 2, 226; Goethe, 1811–4: vol. 3, 290.
[25] Eger, 2025: vol. 1., 535–610; Rocher, 2023; Rocher, 2025.

domain in which Niethammer develops a specific conception of human nature and an ideal of education.

The main implications of Niethammer's "humanism" will be outlined in the paragraphs below, followed by an analysis of his definition to determine if it should be interpreted as the anti-descriptivist first baptism of an as-yet unnamed entity or as merely an attempt to forge a new horizon of thought and a new project.[26]

The Enlightenment was the *first* front to emerge in Niethammer's conception of humanism. He asserted that the emergence of the Enlightenment had compelled the older "spirit of humanism" to make way for it.[27] And exactly what is the Enlightenment, according to Niethammer? – a worldview that is mechanistic and utilitarian. He claimed it had reduced man to a function and to the status of a mere body, a "machine"[28] establishing the foundation for an education that privileged vocational training[29] and "material production"[30] over one grounded in reason. Niethammer claimed that the "great reformer" Frederick II,[31] the Prussian king who propagated the philanthropinist pedagogy of utilitarian education, was responsible for this turn. For whatever reason, however, Niethammer chose not to highlight the rift that had developed among the philanthropinists thirty years prior: between so-called rationalists and the "Alsatians" ("Elsässer"), a group that was similar to the Sturm und Drang movement. It is important to ask to what extent Niethammer's criticism of philanthropinism was a response to, or a reverberation of, this rupture, which ultimately led to the "Alsatians" parting ways with the rationalists and imperiling various disciplines related to philanthropinism.[32]

Niethammer's understanding of the Enlightenment and his anti-Enlightenment position were, however, impactful at that time and precipitated a crucial departure from the Enlightenment ideas of reason and education.

Friedrich Schelling's 1809 review of Niethammer's work contrasts his "modern humanism"[33] with the "gloom of the earlier times and the conceit of a partial Enlightenment, entirely barbaric in its essence, and thus one that springs back to

---

[26] On the confrontation between the performative anti-descriptivism of Saul Kripke and the descriptivism of Slavoj Žižek cf. Laclau, 2005: particularly 101–4; Butler, 1997: Particularly 285–97. On the genealogical concept of the history of names as a whole cf. Bergunder, 2014 = Bergunder, 2011; Bergunder, 2024: 2–8.

[27] Niethammer, 1808: 33–4.

[28] Niethammer, 1808: 43.

[29] Cf. Niethammer, 1808: 188.

[30] Niethammer, 1808: 15.

[31] Niethammer, 1808: 15–6.

[32] Goethe, Herder, Hamann, Lavater, and Jakob Michael Reinhold, for example, were also involved in these disputes between the rationalists around Johann Bernhard Basedow and Joachim Heinrich Campe and the "Alsatians" around Johann Friedrich Simon, Johannes Schweighäuser, Johann Ehrmann, Johann Jakob Mochel, and Christoph Kaufmann Lenz. Cf. on that Eger, 2025: vol. 1, 561–8, 594–7.

[33] Schelling, 1809: 469.

them."[34] In view of the subsequent attempts to parallelize humanism and the Enlightenment or even to equate one with the other, it is important to keep in mind that they were juxtaposed as being opposed to one another from the very start.

Niethammer's *second* frontline does not simply tantamount to the (philosophical) return to a spirit. Rather, it is "the re-Kantianization of idealistic philosophy" or an anthropological accentuation.[35] Niethammer had helped shape that development alongside Fichte, having served as the coeditor of *Philosophisches Journal* in Jena, but he had been spared Fichte's fate in the atheism controversy.[36]

To support his argument, without explicitly citing any specific writings of Kant, Niethammer used an idea fundamental to Kant's critical philosophy: man's "double nature."[37] According to Niethammer, while one dimension of man is a purely spiritual being,[38] the other dimension, the animality[39] of the external, corporeal human, has the potential to degenerate into bestiality[40] under certain conditions unless man's "own guardian spirit" saves him.[41] Niethammer – unlike the unnamed "philosophers of humanity," clearly the idealists and subjectivists[42] – opposed the quest to separate man's spiritual essence from the external visible world of the senses. His mission, as he puts it, was to integrate the "two-fold nature and destiny of man"[43] to allow humanity and animality to permeate one another – to coexist.[44]

Thus, whereas the "Enlightenment" had increasingly aspired to a form of despiritualization ("*Entgeistung*"),[45] Niethammer was more concerned with integration, in fact, with a *third* emphasis. The genuine essence of man, he claimed, does not solely reside in "*pure spirituality*" but, rather, reason urges man to merge his spiritual and animal nature. However, Niethammer clearly believed that, compared to the animal, man definitively belongs to a "*higher spiritual order*,"[46] and human spirituality transcends mere intelligibility and earthly reality and extends to another dimension, notably the afterlife. In this context, the crucial term "soul" is conspicuously absent. Niethammer, a Kantian, may

---

[34] Schelling, 1809: 480.
[35] Frank, 1997: 502, also quoted in Wenz, 2008a: 52.
[36] Cf. in that regard Essen and Danz (eds.), 2012.
[37] Niethammer, 1808: 70.
[38] Cf. Niethammer, 1808: 39.
[39] Cf. Niethammer, 1808: 34.
[40] Cf. Niethammer, 1808: 45–6.
[41] Niethammer, 1808: 47. On the guardian spirit debates that raged around 1800, also by Kant supporters, cf. Stengel, 2011a: 704–21 = Stengel, 2023: 810–29.
[42] Cf. Niethammer, 1808: 41.
[43] Cf. Niethammer, 1808: 45.
[44] Cf. Niethammer, 1808: 67, 70 passim.
[45] Cf. Niethammer, 1808: 18 (emphasized in original).
[46] Niethammer, 1808: 69–70 (emphasized in original).

have been circumventing the notion of soul's immortality, but it is important to ascertain if he had done so consciously. For instance, Niethammer may have distanced himself from a central theme of Enlightenment theology and philosophy in reaction to Schleiermacher's[47] assertion made only a few years prior that the idea that a person's personality endured after death is wholly irreligious. Niethammer never explicitly affirmed that the soul is immortal even though he spoke of man's awareness of a nonearthly reality and his conviction in a greater purpose for the world and a personal life beyond death. I, therefore, address the question of otherworldliness, afterlife, or supernatural destiny as they pertain to this context in the following.

A critical position that Niethammer took was that Enlightenment *and* philanthropinism had instilled in man the "refusal to believe in the invisible,"[48] destroying to such an extent the spiritual side of man that any form of "elevation above the earthly" had been "brought into disrepute *in the name of Enlightenment* [...] as mystical, nonsense belief, anything living in ideas ridiculed as enthusiasm."[49] According to Niethammer, philanthropinism had sought to disabuse children of their faith in what was invisible, even in God himself, probably out of concern that they might embolden them to believe in ghosts, witches, and the devil.[50] Without mentioning any specific names, but with an apparent literal allusion to Kant, Niethammer rejected the demand to focus on the "present calling" and refrain from "raving" about[51] what lay beyond the earthly bounds of existence – an "empty nothingness" or a "new land of joy for mortals in blissful immortality." For him, these "principles" are "categorically irrational and pernicious, dishonoring reason and humanity."[52] In Niethammer's opinion, the "visible" alone does not possess reality. For anyone upholding this conviction,

> having learned to believe in a higher purpose of this world and of life, and with the awareness of a reality other than that of the earth, this life has an entirely different quality of seriousness than one of necessity. Necessity made one petty and mean, whereas the higher purpose elevated man: but the latter alone is known to him who is educated only for the conditional, and to him everything is playfulness unless necessity confronts him with its seriousness.

---

[47] Cf. Schleiermacher, 1799: 130–3, as well as 96–108; cf. on the contextual backdrop to this repudiation, Stengel, 2011b: 159–60; Stengel, 2011a: 718–21 = Stengel, 2023: 826–9; Stengel, 2013d.

[48] Niethammer, 1808: 48.

[49] Niethammer, 1808: 18 (emphasized in original).

[50] Cf. Niethammer, 1808: 58.

[51] Cf. Niethammer, 1808: 50–1; cf. the conclusion of Träume eines Geistersehers, Kant (1902–2022), AA 02: 373, or Kritik der praktischen Vernunft, AA 05: 57; cf. on that Stengel, 2011a: 695–700 = Stengel, 2023: 799–805.

[52] Niethammer, 1808: 51. This phrase is attributed to philanthropists who, while not denying the afterlife, do not see it as a maxim for action in present life.

Those with a higher purpose embrace life with a far nobler sense. A mind raised to heaven by religion sees even the earth in a heavenly light [...]".[53]

This human dimension of an intelligible reason that is oriented toward the hereafter is entirely missing in some of Niethammer's accounts,[54] presumably to allay concerns that a renowned Kantian might have revealed his potentially pre-Enlightenment or pre-critical leanings. After all, Niethammer, like some other enlightened contemporaries, reported sensing the "spiritual presence" of his wife after her death, revealing his vast "experiences of the mind" (*Gemüthserfahrungen*) to prove immortality and the possibility of a reunion in the afterworld, but also seeking to protect himself against accusations of "hard-to-believe speculation."[55] At the latest from then on, Niethammer began referring to himself a mystic – an iridescent term in the early 19th century that was less concerned with medieval authors and more with esoteric currents between spiritism and occultism.[56]

Niethammer's humanism, which emphasizes the supernatural destiny of man, was a crucial component of his pedagogical plan. *Fourthly*, Niethammer was not interested in promoting a particular theological doctrinal system, even though, later, he published Luther's writings,[57] started reforming the educational system in the Lutheran part of Bavaria, where he is still regarded favorably as a Lutheran convert from Kantianism.[58] In his integrative educational project, also known as "philanthropinistic humanism,"[59] Niethammer reveals he had furthermore contemplated a plan to integrate civil society, starting with the notion of a common human supernatural destiny, whereby everyone "learns to recognize themselves as members of one body, as instruments of one reason, and as children of one God".[60] This common supernatural purpose would level out denominationalisms.

Fifth, Niethammer's humanism is notably not just a linguistic educational program. He opposes "mere *verbiage* in pedagogy" and the reduction of philology to the study of *"words and letters."*[61] For Niethammer, language

---

[53] Niethammer, 1808: 101.
[54] This corresponds to the fact that Wenz, 2008a: 111, contented himself with following Niethammer's own assertion that he was averse to "any *awakened* mysticism" (emphasis of the author). The traces have not been investigated, neither here nor in Wenz, 2008b.
[55] Lindner, 1971: 291. Niethammer's letter to Hegel dated July 14, 1832, Lindner, 1971. Wenz simply omits this crucial nuance in Niethammer, citing instead his aversion to the revival movement. Cf. Wenz, 2008a: 111.
[56] On the explicit expectations of reunions that have flourished in scholarly discourse since the end of the 18th century and appear, for example, in this book, which has been published and translated several times: Engel, 1787. See note 41, as well as more comprehensively: Sawicki, 2016.
[57] Niethammer, 1817.
[58] Cf. in contrast Wenz, 2008a: 107–10; Wenz, 2008b: 299, with respect to Lindner's Lutheran position, see note 55.
[59] Wenz, 2008b: 193–98.
[60] Niethammer, 1808: 128.
[61] Niethammer, 1808: 166, 164 (emphasized in original).

education is only a *"means of free education."*[62] His utopic school of thought focused on inculcating reason and edifying humans,[63] and enhancing human intellect[64] through "education" rather than mere "vocational training."[65]

Sixthly, and finally, however, this strand of humanism was not intended to be a rival to or to serve as a substitute for Christianity. In 1808, when Niethammer was contemplating rebuilding the nation, he observed that, whereas the classics had been used to create a sense of national identity in England, France, Italy, and Spain, such "masterpieces" were lacking in Germany.[66] As a way to cultivate a German "national taste" and allow the educational system to gain "practical influence over the entire national education,"[67] Niethammer advocated resorting to "classical works of art of the antiquity," which the "good genius of our good nation" had the ability to effectively curate.[68] Furthermore, the Greco-Roman antiquity does not play a significant role in Niethammer's writings as he did not associate humanism with antiquity, and to that extent, humanism would not have to be revived or recreated parallel to the Renaissance in juxtaposition with the Reformation. Niethammer makes no mention of the Renaissance or the 15th and the 16th centuries. In a similar vein, neither diastasis nor synthesis are represented in Christianity and humanism; in fact, neither position is thematized therein. Niethammer is primarily concerned with moulding the national taste and educating the spiritual side of man – only among other things – through language instruction. In that sense, the "revival" of humanism's spirit connotes a renaissance of a "true philosophical thinking" and the "spirit of humanity" in relation to "animal existence"[69] rather than a return to a classical-philosophical thinking.

Friedrich Schelling emphasized this very point in his critique of Niethammer's proposal: the Greek spirit and Roman culture are not norms that need to be revived or preserved, nor do the Greeks need to be mimicked.[70] Instead, it was deemed important to experience the eternal beauty of their works. Even Schelling did not consider the Renaissance to be the revival of a spirit of the antiquity, nor did he imply that humanism was in any way in conflict with Christianity. Rather, he concurred that this education was intended for the "best of the strong, peculiar people," precisely to prevent duplicating other peoples' experiences. His assertion in the third year following the military disaster of Jena and Auerstedt, that

---

[62] Niethammer, 1808: 221 (emphasized in original).
[63] Cf. Niethammer, 1808: 189.
[64] Cf. Niethammer, 1808: 167.
[65] Cf. Niethammer, 1808: 188–9.
[66] Cf. Niethammer, 1808: 235–6.
[67] Niethammer, 1808: 311.
[68] Niethammer, 1808: 237.
[69] Niethammer, 1808: 33–4.
[70] Cf. Schelling, 1809: 476–7.

one must educate oneself according to "the canon of free and beautiful humanity,"[71] is unambiguously patriotic.

However, seventhly Niethammer asserts that the "education of humankind"[72] serves a higher purpose, one that goes beyond its impact on nation building and on the intelligible and other dimensions of man and humankind, which he believed extended beyond earthly life because of its orientation towards universal reason. A nation that neglects this form of education and only promotes "bread, i.e., vocational sciences" should forfeit its status as a cultural nation, and even cease to be "an active member in the spiritual empire of the education of humankind."[73] This idea suggests that the Kantian Niethammer had adopted Kant's notion of cosmopolitanism.

In view of the reflections rendered below on how humanism had transformed since the 19th century, it is sufficient to note here briefly that Niethammer's humanism served as a counter-concept to the model of Enlightenment education, which he deemed too utilitarian, serving the corporeal here-and-now ends of this world. Niethammer reframed the purpose of education, referring to Kant's intelligible, nondiscursive dimensions of man as "non-normative" – insofar as the intelligible side offered no concrete instructions for action. Two essential characteristics of humanity are emphasized: *first*, the universal capacity of man to reason, highlighted without further explanation in contrast to the idea of purpose and animality, and, *secondly*, the recognition of an intelligible and supernatural reality, in contrast to a reality capable of being grasped sensually. In that sense, non-normative also relates to a human dimension that opposes sensual-corporeal exploitation, vocation, and work. For Niethammer, it also forms the essence of man and humanity and extends beyond this existence, both sensually and temporally. However, the "spirit of humanism"[74] is more than an educational endeavour than just a basic, accessible human trait. And it is seen as a form of spiritualization, an end in itself, and to that extent, as universal progress in relation to linguisticity and education.

1.4 Is Niethammer a Humanist?

The claim that humanism is "an indispensable heuristic tool"[75] would necessitate a study of the writings of Niethammer who coined the notion of humanism in light of the established criteria of "humanism" enumerated in *Enzyklopädie*. First, Niethammer was clearly not invested in the 15th and 16th centuries. He

---

[71] Niethammer, 1808: 480.
[72] Niethammer, 1808: 333 (emphasis removed).
[73] Niethammer, 1808: 359.
[74] Niethammer, 1808: 34 (emphasis removed). The spirit of humanism and the spirit of humanity are different from one another, insofar as the former is directed against philanthropinism and serves humanity as an educational concept (Niethammer, 1808).
[75] Walther, 2007a: 668.

considered humanism both Kantian and anti-Enlightenment. It is assumed that the ancient spirit is merely a foundational supplement for developing national taste and not for reviving a spirit that had purportedly been suppressed by Christianity in the Middle Ages and then revived in the so-called Renaissance. On the one hand, Niethammer's emphasis on the "dual nature of man" is reminiscent of Kant and the philosophical rationalists.[76] Going by the assertion in the *Enzyklopädie* article that humanism sought "earthly reality, moral action, secular ethics, and elegant manners,"[77] Niethammer would have to be excluded entirely from that orbit of humanists. For he asserts that man's essence lies in intelligibility, residing in otherworldliness, and that it has supernatural destiny, however, he does not dispute the necessity of concurrently cultivating and educating man's animalist and human dimensions.

Furthermore, the humanism is portrayed in *Enzyklopädie* as the most important educational movement[78] before the Enlightenment and a forerunner of Niethammer's humanism while also being something Niethammer had rejected. This teleology is revived in 1885, when Friedrich Paulsen named Niethammer the founder of "neohumanism"[79] (although the term does not appear in any of his writings), and in 1921, when an altogether different stage of development is invoked for the first time in Eduard Spranger's notion of "third humanism."[80] For such attributions inexorably essentialize humanism as a pre-existing entity and a handy recourse to ancient anthropologies in the Renaissance, which Niethammer had purportedly brought to life. However, the core criteria attributed to humanism as a suprahistorical phenomenon would necessarily have to apply to Niethammer as well.

Last but not least, Niethammer egregiously neglects to address humanism's special relationship to Christianity and the church, or to explain how it differs from rationalism or even atheism. These connections, some of which will be analyzed in the next section, *after* Niethammer became components of the overarching story of Europe.

According to Niethammer, humanism is categorically neither an era nor a system of doctrines in the history of ideas, and nor is it an epoch that can be historically verified with legitimate claims to historicity that devolved into a suprahistorical program over time. Niethammer views humanism as an ideal of education strongly emphasizing the intelligible side over the merely sensually-conceived conceived machine of the body and links its utilitarian

---

[76] Niethammer, 1808: 58.
[77] Walther, 2007a: 666.
[78] Cf. Walther, 2007a: 665
[79] Cf. Walther, 2009: 136; Walther, 2007b: 702; Liebing, 1986: 159; Lindner, 1971: 224, 244.
[80] Cf. for a more comprehensive analysis on this inconsistent and almost incomprehensible construction, Stiewe, 2011: 4.

anthropology summarily with the Enlightenment. Since it has ramifications for the entire nation, this conception propagates – in final analysis – *its cosmopolitan intention*[81] in the Kantian sense. Niethammer's "humanism," thus, barely fits into the definitions put forth in later lexical entries. At key points, his humanism must be clearly removed from the concepts of humanism in the 19th and 20th centuries.

What conclusions can be drawn for the current debate if even the first and most important architect of humanism cannot credibly be considered a humanist? In spite of Niethammer's putting forth a concept of humanism here, the heuristic benefits of humanism immediately following the baptism of humanism would seem neither plausible nor convincing.

The present Element examines the viability and validity of "humanism" from a historico-critical perspective in view of the normative power of such signifiers as the Enlightenment or humanism, owing to their demarcations from the supposedly unenlightened, non-, anti-, or pre-human in the contemporary hegemonic discourses of power. Beginning with the qualities associated with the concept of humanism *after* its conceptualization, this Element *begins* by tracing the respective connotations and contexts of humanism right up to 1880, which continue to shape debates today.

In addition to examining the central historiographical concept of humanism, *secondly*, the present Element offers a factual and conceptual redefinition of the 15th–16th century literary and cultural phenomenon commonly called as humanism. This provides a necessary corrective alternative to a reading that is currently historiographically anchored. A strict historicization addresses the issue that emerges with the normative application of historiographical categories and enables a more accurate evaluation of the contemporary sources.

Thirdly, this Element considers approaches to humanism despite, and even helped by, the necessary historicization, and the question of how far a critical and ethically motivated contribution to the current discussion about its scope is possible – and necessary – given how profoundly morally and normatively charged this topic is.

2 "Humanism" in the 19th Century: Between Education, Religion, and History

2.1 Humanism in the Enlightenment?

We must first take into consideration the fact that a particular conception of man, purportedly originating in classical antiquity and revived in the 15th and 16th centuries was not labeled "humanism" in the 18th century. But that does

---

[81] Cf. Kant, Idee zu einer allgemeinen Weltgeschichte in weltbürgerlicher Absicht (1784). AA 08: 17–31.

not imply an absence of anthropology such as Herder's *humanitas* (humanity).[82] The issue here is not, in the narrower sense, anthropology's link with the 15th and 16th centuries, with antiquity, or even with how to contextualize it using ideas of education, religion, and history. Other derivations of *humanitas* show other differences. According to Jacob Brucker's formidable history of philosophy, a reform movement between the "Middle Ages" and the Reformation sought to reintroduce Platonism and Aristotelianism to restore the "purity" of the Latin and Greek languages and "reform science." However, a term that is contrasted with the Reformation is philosophy,[83] which is especially associated with the languages and the fine arts. It is claimed that philosophy had been revived after the "abominable decay" of the sciences, which is said to have also rendered the Reformation necessary and thus impacted on the church.[84] Brucker is unaware of the concept of "humanism," and he also does not attribute to these "*Restauratoribus Literarum*, Platonists and other scholars"[85] any kind of anthropology or a current that is critical of or separate from Christianity or religion, whose paradigmatic program, in addition, would have persisted beyond its own time.

In a similar vein, humanism is not mentioned in Zedler's 13th volume of his 1735 *Universallexikon*. Yet it defines related terms like *humaniora* or *humanitatis studia* as historical terms, as the liberal arts for educating the *septem artes*, the higher faculties of the mind.[86] In Zedler, *humanistae* are not what modern dictionaries and encyclopedias would call students and teachers of these arts. Instead, they speak of legal scholars who are knowledgeable about the relevant law from the Greek and Latin "antiquities," and, therefore, mean legal historians.[87] Similarly, Zedler refers to humanity as bourgeois customs and manners, such as "politeness and affability," without considering their anthropological implications: "Hence, in a manner of speaking, it is a humane man who treats everyone in a friendly and affable manner."[88]

It is remarkable, indeed, that Kant, who served as Niethammer's inspiration, makes no mention of humanism at all. He occasionally resorts to "humanity" to denote bourgeois etiquette, such as social graces and well-being, even connoting "communicability and urbanity."[89] Occasionally Kant describes humanity

---

[82] Cf. in particular Johann Gottfried Herder: Briefe zu Beförderung der Humanität. In Herder, 1991.
[83] Brucker, 1731–7: vol. 6 (1735), 1, 4.
[84] Cf. Brucker, 1731–7: vol. 6 (1735), 5.
[85] Brucker, 1731–7: vol. 5 (1734), 1327–8.
[86] Cf. Art. Humaniora oder Humanitatis Studia, 1735: 1155–6; Brucker also uses "Literas humaniores", cf. Brucker, 1731–7: vol. 6 (1735), 30.
[87] Art. Humanistae, 1735: 1156. Goethe might have been referring to this entry, see above, note 24.
[88] Art. Humanität, 1735.
[89] Kant, Logik. AA 09: 46.

as gentleness, for instance in his *Reflections*;⁹⁰ however, his later work, *Metaphysik der Sitten* (Metaphysics of Morals) shows that humanity also derives from his preoccupation with empirical psychology, to mean "affected humanity" (*affectirte Humanität*), which he calls "*compassibilitas*," probably his own neologism, which he describes in greater detail.⁹¹ If *compassibilitas* and "communicability" encompass such human qualities as compassion, empathy and communicability, perhaps another late passage in Kant's *Anthropologie in pragmatischer Hinsicht* (Anthropology from a Pragmatic Point of View) points to the connection between a putative eudaemonistic doctrine of happiness in the Wolffian sense and the rules of morality prescribed in the categorical imperative. Here, humanity implies "a way to conceptualize that combines living well with virtue in practice."⁹² Yet Kant clearly uses a non-normative definition of *humanitas* in his *Grundlegung zur Metaphysik der Sitten* (Groundwork of the Metaphysics of Morals) rather than using the term in a way that has historical or religious connotations. He describes it as an assessment of human capabilities at the level of basic anthropological constants: as *humanitas* without a modifier. Niethammer may have drawn a distinction between humanity and animality based on the idea that man is not just rational but also an animal endowed with the capacity for reason. Kant distinguishes between *humanitas practica*, which refers to the ability and the willingness to communicate "feelings" with one another, from *humanitas aesthetica*, or man's "receptivity to the shared experience of pleasure or pain."⁹³ However, that does not represent a normative moral claim for humanity, but frames only the basic human configuration and disposition. Even Kant's distinction in his preliminary work towards his *Metaphysics* cannot transcend that: "*Humanitas substantialis* [means] humankind [Menschheit]; [*humanitas*] *accidentalis* [means] humanity [Menschlichkeit]."⁹⁴

Thus, it is remarkable that the thinker who had a significant impact on Niethammer does not view humanity as a historical-theoretical concept, nor as an educational concept, or as having any connection to classical antiquity or Christianity. In fact, Kant does not define humanity as a distinctly normative

---

⁹⁰ Kant, R 1531 (Anthropologie, most probably 1797). Kant, AA 15: 957.
⁹¹ Kant, AA 06: 335 (referring to Cesare Beccaria's rejection of the death penalty in Dei Delitti E Delle Pene, 1764). Compassibilitas is *Hapax legomenon* in Kant, further proof cannot be provided at the moment. It is conceivable that Kant came up with the concept of humanity through his preoccupation with Herder's *Ideen zur Philosophie der Geschichte der Menschheit* [Ideas for the Philosophy of a History of Mankind]. The term appears eight times in Kant's review, notably also in the understanding of religion as the highest form of humanity. Kant, AA 08: 45–52, here 49.
⁹² Kant, AA 07: 277.
⁹³ Kant, AA 06: 456.
⁹⁴ Kant, Preliminary works on the preface and introduction to the doctrine of virtue in the Metaphysics of Morals. AA 13: 398.

idea or as falling within the purview of humanism as it is understood today and since the 19th century since he does not categorize this fivefold connotation differently. In any case, Niethammer's humanism differs significantly from the way Enlightenment thinkers viewed humanity. Instead, it reinforces the sharp distinction that Niethammer – and Schelling – made between humanism and the Enlightenment.

2.2 World Spirit instead of Pedagogy: Hegel

In the decades after Niethammer first proposed the concept of humanism, it was only ever used within the semantic framework he had developed, namely, as a pedagogical (counter-) concept, and not linked to the contemporary philosophical-theological or historiographical debates. Hegel, on rare occasions, used the term "Humanität" – never "humanism" – in a way similar to Kant's *humanitas accidentalis*, which he understood to be humanity on the one hand. For on the other, in contrast to Kant and with reference to Virgil and Horace, Hegel also took humanity to mean something that is comprehensively human or the humankind residing in man, which gods do not possess.[95] Like Kant, Hegel is aware of the connection between "humanity and urbanity," but now sees it as a part of the ancient Greek past, along with Socrates and Plato.[96] In his Jena writings, Hegel contrasts humanity with "hardness" (to imply gentleness/tenderness), in a manner similar to Kant's notion of humanity,[97] but without anchoring his notion of humanity within an epoch. Instead, Hegel's humanity is part of a triangle built in conjunction with freedom and justice, echoing an attitude or quality. Elsewhere it is ascribed normativity, which Hegel rejects: If the absolute master artificer in history, the eternal absolute idea, which realizes itself in mankind, emerges not as a "veiled ongoing necessity" but as an active individual, then either that would shatter the notion of individuality or the idea of the "determination of the human race and its education by achieving humanity, moral perfection, or however else the purpose of world history [...] would sink."[98] If this presumes that Hegel considered the above-mentioned connection between Niethammer's idea of humanism and the higher purpose of human education, then it is one he vehemently opposed. Niethammer's pedagogical idealism is opposed to the

---

[95] G. W. F. Hegel, *Vorlesungen über die Philosophie der Religion*. In Hegel, 1969–81: vol. 17 (1969), 166.

[96] G. W. F. Hegel, *Rechts-, Pflichten- und Religionslehre für die Unterklasse*. In Hegel, 1969–81: vol. 4 (1970), 272.

[97] G. W. F. Hegel, *Über die wissenschaftlichen Behandlungsarten des Naturrechts, seine Stelle in der praktischen Philosophie und sein Verhältnis zu den positiven Rechtswissenschaften*. In Hegel, 1969–81: vol. 2 (1970), 498.

[98] G. W. F. Hegel, *Vorlesungen über die Ästhetik*. In Hegel, 1969–81: vol. 15 (1970), 356–7.

historically necessary development of world spirit. Likewise, the idea of humanity is only tangentially present in Hegel. A "spirit of humanity" in Niethammer's sense would be rejected – from the perspective of world spirit.

2.3 Humanism: Between Realism, 'Christianism', and the Nation

In the years following Niethammer, humanism was particularly embraced by authors within the pedagogical sphere of upper secondary education. In this pedagogical debate, the counter-movement of Philanthropinism was replaced by terms such as Realism or naturalist education. 'Realism' in this context does not refer to the philosophical doctrine but rather pertains to the emphasis on teaching about real-world phenomena, as seen in subjects like geography, history, natural sciences, and natural history. In his commemorative pamphlet for Lessing's 100th birthday, a professor at Meissen's Landesschule Sankt Afra reiterated the coexistence of humanistic and naturalist education in his defense of humanism.[99] Like Niethammer, he also advocated for the simultaneous study of classical antiquity.[100] As early as 1829, the philosopher Wilhelm Braubach, Giessen school director and a student of Johann Heinrich Pestalozzi, promoted the notion of reconciling realism and humanism,[101] viewing the latter merely as a formal principle of language instruction, like Niethammer, to thereby "unlock the treasures of ancient antiquity in the relics of their great minds."[102]

In the same year, 1829, Friedrich Wilhelm Klumpp reinvoked the idea of humanism that Niethammer had introduced twenty years earlier. Klumpp, a senior counselor in Stuttgart, was an adherent of the Württemberg missionary and revivalist movement,[103] and opposed pedagogical humanism. He rejected the call to study language and classical antiquity to educate the "mind for the ideal life." Instead, he privileged realism founded on general science education.[104] Although familiar with philanthropinism,[105] Klumpp expanded the general idea of education beyond Niethammer's emphasis on the nationalist and universalist aspirations of humanism and extended that definition to imbue his brand of humanism with the religious inflection of Christianity towards a "humanism underpinned by Christian and nationalist aspirations."[106] Like Niethammer, Klumpp had previously emphasized that culture corresponded to the progress of the human spirit, adding later it was also predicated on

---

[99] Cf. Diller, 1841: 79.
[100] Cf. Diller, 1841: 76.
[101] Cf. Braubach, 1833: 30.
[102] Braubach, 1833: 4.
[103] Cf. Klumpp, 1844.
[104] Cf. Klumpp, 1829–30: vol. 1, 2.
[105] Cf. Klumpp, 1829–30: vol. 2, 4.
[106] Klumpp, 1829–30: vol. 1, 13.

"Christianity and the basic Germanic character."[107] This nexus would thus allow the Germanic (national) character and Christian principles to foray into Niethammer's semantic field underlying the concept of humanism, which aimed to achieve its national and universal aspirations notwithstanding its pedagogical impetus in contrast to classical education. The links between Christianity, realism, and Germanism had produced clear shifts and extensions.

A book published in the same year (1829) in Leipzig, entitled "Humanism. A Preliminary Text: Nature, Animal, Human, Angel, God," bore verifiable similarities to Niethammer but did not explicitly mention him by name. It claimed that it characterized "only natural philosophy of the natural human being,"[108] specifically emphasizing its intermediate position, constrained by the aforementioned genres of the spirit. Man was contrasted with the animal kingdom and presented as a dual entity comprising both spirit and sensuality[109] on the basis of the assertion that "*theoria, idea*," the actual science underlying it, relied "solely on seeing God."[110] The author's concept of religion unequivocally derived from Schleiermacher and postulated a more distinct knowledge of individuality[111] with a definite orientation to Christ, the human burden of sin, and an infinite separation from God.[112] It concurrently also underscored his belief in the "free grace of God in Christ."[113] This anthropology, clearly soteriological at its foundation, was occasionally referred to as humanism. However, what cannot be clarified is the question of whether the author sought to bridge or overcome a conflict between Christianity and humanism that already existed, and to which conception he was referring in so doing.

Although no other works on humanism had appeared up to this date, by 1830 humanism and Christianity were clearly linked as two autonomous categories, reconciled, or at least symbiotically intertwined.

2.4 The Beginning of a Relationship: Humanism and the Reformation

With the publication of a Thuringian pastor, Wilhelm Schröter, entitled *Christianismus, Humanismus und Rationalismus in ihrer Identität. Ideen zur Beurtheilung der Reformation Luthers und des in ihr wahrhaft Symbolischen*

---

[107] Klumpp, 1829–30: vol. 1, 11. Cf. Bemerkungen zu Herrn Prof. Klumpp's Schrift: Die gelehrten Schulen nach den Grundsätzen des wahren Humanismus und den Anforderungen der Zeit. Von einem Freunde der vaterländischen Schulen, 1829.
[108] Cf. Schüler, 1829: xi.
[109] Cf. Schüler, 1829: xxi. Notwithstanding the title, angels are not a point of discussion.
[110] Schüler, 1829: xvii.
[111] Cf. Schüler, 1829: 39, 114.
[112] Cf. Schüler, 1829: 44–6.
[113] Schüler, 1829: 180.

(Christianism, Humanism and Rationalism in Their Identity. Ideas for the Evaluation of Luther's Reformation and the Truly Symbolic in it), a new semantic field emerged as early as[114] 1831 anticipating central components of humanism that would subsequently converge in the concept from a historical, theological, and philosophical standpoint. Especially remarkable in this context, notwithstanding differentiations between 'Christianism', humanism, and rationalism, is the first mention of Luther. As noted by current scholarship, this emphasizes humanism's connection to the history of the Reformation. Schröter sought to overcome a presumed split between the three mentioned currents through Lutheran Christianity by bringing together the "essence of Christianity" and the "essence of man," which his contemporaries had dismissed as an "ignoble" dispute between "supernaturalists and rationalists."[115] Schröter, on the other hand, equated "Christianism" with Jesus Christ, referring to him as the "real ideal human" and the "ideal human revealed" in him.[116]

This obvious attempt to Christianize a humanistic understanding that was already directed against a specific confessional Christianity also had an anti-Catholic bias, for it believed that although the Catholic Church considered humanism a "nonentity," the "divine" and the "spirit of God in the Reformation had gloriously revealed Luther's inner life."[117] Schröter made no distinction between "Christianism" and the "essence of humanism," asserting: "Humanism is identical to Christianism."[118] Separating Christianism from humanism would inevitably result in a "false idea of humanism."[119] Schröter's understanding of humanism is embossed in his criticism of the then partisans of theological rationalism, Karl von Hase and Philipp Konrad Marheineke.[120]

Schröter's belief that Socrates was a more perfect Christian than some Romans and Protestants had an impact starting with the *Logos-spermatikos* speculation right up to Hermeticism in the 15th century. According to him, Socrates had "humanized or Christianized" his paganism through reason,[121] and he extended this equivalence to Luther, recognizing his "reformatory rationalism," on the one hand, for identifying Christianity with humanism. On the other, he also regarded him as an intellect that had been inspired by Christ, allowing him to emancipate

---

[114] In previous studies, the counterpart of an epochal understanding of humanism to Christianity as the Reformation was first identified in 1841/43 (Spitz) or also in 1859/80 (Walther). This will be pursued further below. Cf. Spitz, 1986: 639; Walther, 2007a: 666. Cf. below note 132.
[115] Schröter, 1831: iv–v. In German, "Christianismus" is a neologism in contrast to "Christentum" and apparently owes its origin to the parallel "Humanismus."
[116] Schröter, 1831: 11–3.
[117] Schröter, 1831: 26, 3.
[118] Schröter, 1831: 31.
[119] Schröter, 1831: 23.
[120] Cf. Schröter, 1831: 42–3.
[121] Schröter, 1831: 107. As a result, Socrates' paganism was said to have become a dead shell.

himself from the religious teachings of the Augustinians.[122] It is evident that for Schröter, drawing a boundary against Augustinianism was crucial, and he did so by identifying rationality with (non-Catholic/Protestant) Christianity.

2.5 Humanism in the Luther Canon? Luther and Erasmus according to Niethammer

While maintaining that Christianism, rationalism, and humanism were intertwined, Wilhelm Schröter explicitly referred to Luther's *De servo arbitrio*. It was not common practice to invoke this particular work which came to be deemed later as unequivocally 'anti-humanist'. Particularly from the 20th century onward, Erasmus was elevated to the status of a 'Prince of the Humanists.' In 1524, Erasmus sharply critiqued Luther's anthropology and hermeneutics in *De libero arbitrio*, first by highlighting the incoherence and historical nature of the biblical canon, and second by emphasizing human freedom and the capacity for synergy in justification – positions that stood in opposition to Luther's view of humans as radically fallen into sin, a perspective he particularly articulated in his theses in the Heidelberg Disputation of 1518.[123] In 1525, Luther responded to Erasmus with *De servo arbitrio*, asserting not only the unequivocal authority of Scripture but also emphasizing divine predestination to such an extent that he denied any human synergy in the act of justification – famously characterizing humans as a horse ridden either by the Devil or by God. This confrontation later became a symbol of the radical rupture between Reformation and Humanism. It posed a dilemma for Reformation and Luther scholars in the 19th century, paralleling the debates surrounding humanism.[124] Leopold von Ranke, in his monumental *Deutsche Geschichte im Zeitalter der Reformation* (German History in the Age of the Reformation), disregarded this work and refrained from mentioning the conflict between Luther and Erasmus.[125] Niethammer himself, who published a collection of Luther's writings in 1817 to mark the 300th anniversary of the nailing of his theses, mentions Reuchlin, Melanchthon, and Erasmus, without labelling them as humanists. Again, Luther's *De servo arbitrio* is not mentioned in Niethammer's study, which is equally notable for the absence of any reference to the anthropological disagreements between Erasmus and Luther.[126] Johann Georg Plochmann's preface to it, carrying a rather detailed overview of Luther's

---

[122] Schröter, 1831: 144, 151.
[123] Cf. Stengel, 2013c; Stengel 2018.
[124] Cf. Schröter, 1831: 152–7, with extensive quotations, including the famous "mount" passage: Man is ridden either by God or by the devil.
[125] Cf. Ranke, 1839–47. In Ranke, Erasmus appears as "the first great author of the opposition in the modern sense," Ranke, 1839–47: vol. 1 (1839), 264. The controversy between Erasmus and Luther is not mentioned.
[126] Cf. Niethammer, 1817.

life for the 65-volume Erlangen edition of Luther's works in 1826, also did not convey any familiarity with the concept of humanism. Nor did he deign to mention Erasmus.[127] The subject index of this 1857 edition contains no entry for *humanism*, but it does now cite Luther's *De servo arbitrio*, the work that Erasmus allegedly was unable to refute.[128] Missing from this colossal edition of Luther's works is his *De servo arbitrio*. Even Hans Lorenz Andreas Vent's preface to the Hamburg Luther edition does not mention *De servo arbitrio*.[129] Not until 1840, when Gustav Pfitzer's popular single-volume Luther edition, compressed into 1500 pages, was published did this work received a mention – but without any allusion to humanism.[130]

It is strikingly odd how confessional studies on Luther in the first half of the 19th century tended to ignore the Erasmus controversy. And the question is if that had anything to do with Erasmus's understanding of "humanity"[131] and Niethammer's concept of humanism, which was resolutely based on the notion of a free and rational human being, and to that extent could hardly be harmonized with Luther's *De servo arbitrio*. How and in what contexts did these references begin to collide? At what point, exactly, can we speak of "humanism" ever merging with the Renaissance philosophy, especially the Erasmian philosophy, to form an anthropological paradigm either as representing Reformation Christianity or its antipode?

2.6 Humanism as Science, Spirit, and Epoch Next to the Reformation: Hagen

I have argued that humanism continued to vacillate between education and anthropology until the German *Vormärz* – the years before the revolution of 1848 – and yet, regardless of how it related to Christianity – but neither as an epoch and nor as a spirit that would have originated in antiquity, achieving historical significance only subsequently. The rupture in the debates become obvious at the latest when Schröter tried to reconcile the differences between Christianity and humanism. Recent research indicates this does not apply to the first mention of humanism as a movement in the early modern period.

Ludwig Wachler's "History of Literature" published in 1823 draws a parallel between the struggles of humanism and mysticism against "scholastic dogmatism" from the mid-15th century until the early 16th century. Humanism is not

---

[127] Cf. Plochmann, 1826b: v–xii; Plochmann, 1826a: 1–66.
[128] Plochmann, 1826a: 66, 217.
[129] Cf. Vent, 1827: iii–xvi.
[130] Cf. Luther, 1840: 645–751.
[131] Cf. e.g. Erasmus von Rotterdam, 1995c: 367, 447 passim, and in the complete works. Cf. still: Raumer, 1953: 1–21.

just associated with classical languages, aesthetics, and imagination. It is also intimately related to the possibility of asserting the "most sacred rights and claims of the more mature human race against the provincial stubbornness of the guild comrades battling for their sole dominance over the mind and science."[132] Erasmus and Reuchlin, representatives of the "dawn of humanistic intellectual formation,"[133] also receive a mention, however, only in relation to the humanistic linguistic studies in the narrower sense,[134] often distinguished from the "realistic stream."[135] Wachler emphasized classical languages in his conception of humanism, appearing to support Niethammer's point of view.[136]

The more precise path must remain unlit for the time being. It lies between Wachler, Schröter (1831), and Karl Hagen, namely the author who was the first to comprehensively conceptualize humanism as a movement since the 15th/16th centuries and as a distinct current alongside the Reformation and clearly neglected by Wachler.[137] Like Wilhelm Zimmermann,[138] Hagen was a theologian and Reformation historian, more specifically a "progressive historian in the *Vormärz*." He served as a lecturer and professor in Heidelberg from 1838 until 1849, and in 1848 the city sent him to the National Assembly. In three volumes that were published at the same time as Ranke's Magnum opus and Zimmermann's mammoth history of the Peasants' War, he presents his perspective on the history of the Reformation as a "radical democrat and political educator,"[139] a fact he himself[140] admitted was strange. Hagen identifies three strands of "opposition"[141] or "oppositional strands"[142] – popular, religious, and humanistic[143] – that gradually converged, mainly on issues relating to the ecclesiastical situation,[144] Rome[145] and scholasticism.[146] Like Niethammer,

---

[132] Wachler, 1822–4: vol. 2 (1823), 246, 259, 262–3. Humanism differs from Platonism, Hermeticism and the Kabbalah of Ficino, Plethon and Pico della Mirandola, Wachler, 1822–4: 263. The later volumes track the humanistic studies through language teaching up to the 18th century, cf. vol. 4 (1824), 56, 62 passim. Baab was first to demonstrate Wachler's use of the concept of humanism, cf. Baab, 2013: 33–4.

[133] Wachler, 1822–4: vol. 4 (1824), 30.

[134] Cf. Wachler, 1822–4: vol. 4 (1824), 9–11, 17–8.

[135] Wachler, 1822–4: vol. 4 (1824), 25.

[136] Niethammer's dispute between philanthropinism and humanism is explicitly mentioned. Cf. Wachler, 1822–4: vol. 4 (1824), 197.

[137] The explicit conceptual significance of Hagen's concept of humanism is underestimated in Baab, who apparently did not take note of vol 3. Baab, 2013: 34–5.

[138] Zimmermann, 1841–3, many edn, most recent (11th ed.) Berlin (GDR) 1989.

[139] Cf. Mühlpfordt, 1980; Wolgast, 1985.

[140] Hagen, 1841–4: vol. 1 (1841), vi.

[141] Hagen, 1841–4: vol. 1 (1841), 377.

[142] Hagen, 1841–4: vol. 1 (1841), 32.

[143] Cf. Hagen, 1841–4: vol. 1 (1841), 32.

[144] Cf. Hagen, 1841–4: vol. 1 (1841), 364.

[145] Cf. Hagen, 1841–4: vol. 1 (1841), 475.

[146] Cf. Hagen, 1841–4: vol. 1 (1841), 278.

supporters of the humanistic school, some even ardent opponents of the church, pursued the study of classical languages.[147] That is when humanism comes to mean "seeds of the newer scientific strand," while elsewhere it is associated with the scientific direction generally taken by the opposition.[148] In the process, when Luther was grouped with Erasmus, Reuchlin, and Pico della Mirandola, among others,[149] the Reformation had effectively "united the popular, humanist, religious adversaries."[150] In that sense, humanism came to be revered as an educational movement, aiming to integrate the "education of the mind and the heart,"[151] and to that extent exceeded the scope of merely being the study of language in Niethammer's assessment.

For the first time, humanism gains a distinct position in relation to religion, as a science with an educational impetus. Also, for the first time, it becomes possible to identify Hagen's claim that Italian "humanism" was distinct from its German counterpart in how it expressed its indifference towards Christianity and the church: Erasmus, for example, is believed to have espoused the "freer strand of Christian theology."[152] One nation is described as having a "synthetic" relationship with humanism as science, education, and theology, whereas the other is merely "indifferent" in this regard. In this spectrum of interpretations, "humanism" begins to emerge as a historical force.

In the preface to the second volume of his Reformation history, Hagen emphasized his efforts to subsume numerous historical oppositional currents under one category. He rejected all previous attempts to interpret the Reformation only from the perspective of Protestant church doctrine, which would have disregarded or "obliquely" evaluated such "endeavors" that did not conform to Protestant church doctrine or were categorically opposed to it.[153] Then Hagen made a distinction between Protestantism, as it had evolved in the churches since the 16th century, and the grander, more significant, and more comprehensive "original tendency of the Reformation"[154] that transcended Protestantism. Instead of the three currents mentioned in the first volume, he was now aware of an opposition at the national level and the "opposition of the humanists" alongside Luther and his adversaries from Leipzig.[155] To create

---

[147] Cf. Hagen, 1841–4: vol. 1 (1841), 39, 79.
[148] Hagen, 1841–4: vol. 1 (1841), 99, 208.
[149] Hagen, 1841–4: vol. 1 (1841), 232–3, 256, 464.
[150] Hagen, 1841–4: vol. 1 (1841), 377.
[151] Hagen, 1841–4: vol. 1 (1841), 279.
[152] Cf. Hagen, 1841–4: vol. 1 (1841), 323.
[153] Cf. Hagen, 1841–4: vol. 2 (1843), ix.
[154] Hagen, 1841–4: vol. 2 (1843), x.
[155] Hagen, 1841–4: vol. 2 (1843), 27, 47.

a common front in the republican sense, Hagen may have imported the ideological front lines from the 1840s into his analysis.

However, both in 1843 and in the third volume that came out in 1844, Hagen refined his history of the Reformation into a general critique of Protestantism. Now he regarded Protestantism as a "deviant variant" (*Abart*) of the actual and original essence of the Reformation, to which he had expressed his indifference, seeking to portray it just as "ruthlessly" as he had the Catholic Church.[156] Now, oppositional movements synthesized in the previous volumes were portrayed as "oppositional movements within the Reformation movement."[157] In addition to a whole range of conflicts, the dispute between Erasmus and Luther is taken up conspicuously in parallel to the inclusion of this debate in the popular Luther canon.

Nonetheless, the "freer faction of the opposition" is the focus of attention.[158] It is argued that the advocates of this faction, where popular, religious, and humanistic ideas had converged to form an impressive cluster, represent the true "Reformation spirit."[159] Until the historiographies of the 21st century, this group oscillates between "humanists," Hermetics, Spiritualists, and especially Anabaptists. The democratic opponent Hagen apparently regarded them as his spiritual ancestors. The three volumes present the pinnacle and the culmination of the Reformation movement, with "Sebastian Franck, the forerunner of modern German philosophy."[160] Franck, who was part of both the opposition's freer faction and the Reformation faction, came to be regarded as a "forerunner of a new trajectory in the human spirit."[161] Hagen's analysis of the contentious relationship between the "new orthodoxy"[162] and other Reformation currents, particularly humanism, is vital at this juncture. As the narrative goes, the alliance between the Reformation orthodoxy and humanists to forge the Reformation spirit broke down when the new orthodoxy was formed, but the "humanistic element" endured despite the opposition and neglect of the reformers.[163] The "less" free biblical faction persisted with their mystical preoccupations, for example, through Jakob Böhme. The non-free faction, on the other hand, would have "preferred to appropriate the Reformation or Protestantism as their own."[164] The three factions, the free mystical or

---

[156] Hagen, 1841–4: vol. 3 (1844), vii.
[157] Based on the title of the entire first chapter in Hagen, 1841–4: vol. 3 (1844), 1–141.
[158] Hagen, 1841–4: vol. 3 (1844), 314.
[159] Hagen, 1841–4: vol. 3 (1844), 246–7. Hagen mentions, among others, Erasmus, Agrippa von Nettesheim, Christoph Fürer, Hans Denck, Ludwig Hätzer, Johann Bünderlin, Johann Campanus, Michael Servet, and the Anabaptists at many junctures
[160] Hagen, 1841–4: vol. 3 (1844), 314–96.
[161] Hagen, 1841–4: vol. 3 (1844), 314.
[162] This is the title of the entire second chapter in Hagen, 1841–4: vol. 3 (1844), 142–200.
[163] Cf. Hagen, 1841–4: vol. 3 (1844), 459–61.
[164] Hagen, 1841–4: vol. 3 (1844), 459.

rationalistic (!), the humanistic, and the "national popular," were reunited in the 18th century and gave rise to a "tremendous upswing in the spirit and the literature of our people," "which is still benefiting us."[165]

Whether Niethammer's definition of humanism forms the basis of humanism as redefined by Karl Hagen will be addressed at a later point. The well-known opposition of humanism and mysticism to scholasticism, humanism's ties to antiquity, and the ideal of a "more mature"[166] human being are all examples of Wachler's influence. Yet neither Hagen nor Wachler identified a fundamental distinction or conflict between humanism and Christianity. The early modern reference to "mere language education" and *humanistas* was no longer present in Hagen.

Hagen's new combination of humanism, education, history, and religion consisted firstly in the fact that humanism clashed with the essence of the Reformation, secondly that humanism was expressed in the anthropological conflict between Erasmus and Luther, and thirdly that, as a scientific and at the same time free-spirited movement, humanism transported the true spirit of the Reformation as opposed to (state) Protestantism and Pietism as an orthodoxy (!) in Hagen's work.[167]

Hagen sees humanism, as a spirit that evolved into history, was capable of fusing briefly with other forces, but it ultimately conveyed the "ideals of freedom and humanity,"[168] which Hagen believed had been lost in the political skirmishes of the *Vormärz*. For Hagen, humanism is both a Christian and pedagogical force, an entity that has become history and is always at work through history, especially through its opposition to the Reformation, first symbiotically and then through more over conflicts.

Hagen became active in reform education through his connections to Friedrich Fröbel and Johann Heinrich Pestalozzi,[169] eventually advocating for free schools and propagating "humanism" as a means to educate and engage in political critique. Humanism was neither directed against Christianity nor was it irreligious; it advocated for the spiritualist-"humanist" tradition to challenge the contemporary statist orthodoxy. In a work titled *Über Nationale Erziehung* (On National Education), published in 1845, Fröbel described humanism as a movement that had existed since the 14th century, which influenced taste through the study of ancient languages and secularization and had come into conflict with reformers despite initially garnering their support.[170] It is possible

---

[165] Hagen, 1841–4: vol. 3 (1844), 461. The keyword "Enlightenment" is not used here, however.
[166] Wachler, 1822–4: vol. 2 (1823), 263.
[167] Hagen, 1841–4: vol. 3 (1844), 462.
[168] Hagen, 1841–4: vol. 3 (1844), 458.
[169] Cf. Hagen, 1948: 99–100.
[170] Hagen, 1948: 101–3.

that Hagen had only indirectly alluded to Niethammer through Johann Bernhard Basedow. He characterized pedagogy's decline to the level of "practicality" and "utility" by drawing a distinction between Basedow's "realism" and the humanism. Furthermore, this integration reached its peak toward the end of the 18th century when Kant's philosophy and Pestalozzi's notion of the "education of the whole person" were both absorbed by humanism. Hagen once again underlined the anti-church and anti-dogmatic bent of his scientific humanism by opposing mandatory religious instruction altogether, claiming – in reference to the United States – that, among other things, religious education incited "hatred."[171] Hagen might have completed a first circle by asserting that humanism was a historical movement concurrent with the Reformation, noting Niethammer's emphasis on pedagogy, which Fröbel and Pestalozzi had successfully employed.

Furthermore, Hagen's humanism must be distinguished from Leopold von Ranke's since Ranke paid less attention to the Luther-Erasmus controversy than Hagen. He also did not view humanism as a concept even while proclaiming that "familiarity" with classical antiquity had been the "most powerful inner drive" for the "German spirit"[172] at the beginning of the 16th century. However, while Ranke found no conflict between antiquity and the Reformation and considered them harmonious, Hagen argued that humanism was opposed to the church – although not to Christianity.

2.7 Humanism as an Interlude: Marx, Engels, Marxism

Karl Hagen's "humanism" was a pedagogical concept rooted in the German *Vormärz*. It was politically charged, alternatively religious and critical of the church, and projected contemporary battle lines back to the 15th/16th centuries. Many left-leaning Hegelian authors used humanism as a complement to socialist theories. In *Heilige Familie* (The Holy Family) (1844), Marx and Engels refer to humanism as Hagen had redefined it in response to earlier disputes at the beginning of the 1840s, and in so doing they suggest a materialist understanding of humanism:

> Real humanism has no more dangerous enemy in Germany than spiritualism or speculative idealism, which substitutes "self-consciousness" or the "spirit" for the real individual and teaches with the evangelist: "It is the spirit that makes alive, the flesh is of no use". It is understood that this fleshless spirit has spirit only in his imagination.[173]

---

[171] Hagen, 1948: 124–6.
[172] Ranke, 1839–47: vol. 5 (1843), 465.
[173] John 6,63; Marx and Engels, Die heilige Familie (September 1844). MEW 02: 3–223, here 7 (Vorrede/Preface).

What humanism means is not explicitly explained. Instead, it is distinguished from spiritualism, perhaps in light of contemporary debates on spiritualism,[174] and idealism, the latter obviously in reference to Fichte and the idealist Hegelian opponents.

That same year, however, humanism earned several mentions in Marx's *Ökonomisch-philosophische Manuskripte* (Economic and Philosophic Manuscripts) (1844). Approaching humanism more meticulously, he distinguished it from idealism and materialism, and sometimes equated it with naturalism.[175] At the same time, he linked humanism to atheism and communism, implying that atheism was synonymous with the "coming of age of theoretical humanism" with its demand for the abolition of God, while communism represented the "coming of age of practical humanism."[176] In this work, humanism serves as a generic term for the theory and practice of the Marxist historical and philosophical project as a human-centered philosophy that strives for fulfillment. This connotation was radically new: humanism was now associated with atheism and no longer considered as being merely critical of the church. This meant that the religious and alternative-Christian meaning of the term claimed by all authors before had not only been supplemented but liquidated. At a critical juncture, it had been reinscribed as a signifier into a fundamentally different interpretative context, departing from earlier meanings that were partially complementary. The claim of some authors, including Michael Schmidt-Salomon, that Marx had called for a "categorical imperative of humanism," has been systematically refuted as an erroneous conflation of Kant's moral philosophy with Marx's short-lived use of the concept of humanism.[177]

First, however, it should be noted that the atheistic conceptualization was not upheld in communist literature, as the concept that had been so significant just before did not simply disappear with the publication of *Manifest der Kommunistischen Partei* (Communist Manifesto) in 1848. The philanthropists *and* the humanists were now being categorically labeled as those whose efforts to resolve "social grievances" aimed to support bourgeois society.[178] From that point on, the communist movement increasingly embraced this rejection of "revisionist" or petty-bourgeois reformers. In a decisive move, the *Manifesto*

---

[174] Cf. on the distinction between spiritism and spiritualism, which was only made in the context of Alan Kardec's Buch der Geister and overall Sawicki, 2016: 267–96 passim; within the frame of reference of spiritualism, Stengel, 2013b.

[175] Cf. Marx, Ökonomisch-philosophische Manuskripte (Erste Wiedergabe). MEGA I.2: 187–322, here 295; Zweite Wiedergabe, 323–438, here 389, 408.

[176] MEGA I.2: 301 (Erste Wiedergabe).

[177] Cf. Baab, 2013: 159, 191.

[178] Marx and Engels, Manifest der Kommunistischen Partei. Grundsätze des Kommunismus (1848). MEW 04: 461–93, here 488.

united two groups that had been dichotomized since Niethammer as those who sought to educate without transforming social relations, especially the power and property relations: the reformist educational faction of humanists *and* the philanthropists.

Marx and Engels offered an explanation for this humanist interlude in the early communist movement four years later. In *Die großen Männer des Exils* (Heroes of the Exile), they reckoned with the former left Hegelian partisan, Arnold Ruge, who, only a few years earlier, had rescued humanism, which had served as "the phrase that all confusionists in Germany, from Reuchlin to Herder, have used to cloak their embarrassment." Ruge had allegedly clung to it with "desperation," insisting that humanism still held sway in Germany.[179]

For all intents and purposes, the founders of Marxism had rejected the idea of humanism that had been central to Ruge's vision for society as idealistic, an alternative to religion, but above all as nonmaterialist and capable of merging the pedagogical and socialist dimensions. Although it is unclear if Marx and Engels had entirely rejected humanism in response to how Ruge used it, the conflict between the two was already imminent in 1843/44.[180]

Moses Hess, briefly an ally of Ruge and Marx, was a significant left Hegelian author in the humanism controversy. Hess claimed in 1844 that humanism was the "essential German element," indeed the "essence"[181] of German philosophy in general and that it had "evolved" alongside "socialism" in Germany since 1843 (!), whereas French socialism had given rise to practical humanism. Since then, the "best minds in Germany have been won over by socialism."[182] Hess believed that true humanism was a "doctrine of man" and of human society that included both theory and practice. He shared Feuerbach's perspective that theology is anthropology. However, going beyond Feuerbach, he emphasized "the social essence" and the shared aim of different individuals, adding that true humanism is consequently the "doctrine of the human social order, meaning that anthropology is socialism".[183] As with Marx, the principles of humanism and social justice are, indeed, harnessed in communism;[184] however, the extent to which Karl Hagen's conception was reflected here remains to be explored.

---

[179] Marx and Engels, Die großen Männer des Exils (1852). MEW 08: 233–335, here 278 (emphasized in original); cf. Baab, 2013: 45.

[180] Cf. Kiesewetter, 2011: 33. Around 1845, Max Stirner also used "humanism" as an antonym to egoism in a few places, as a complementary term to communism, as a substitute term for the ancient Greek sophistry and as a counterterm to the Reformation and Christianity (!). Cf. Stirner, 1845: 34, 413.

[181] Cf. Hess, 1961: 286.

[182] Hess, 1961: 304.

[183] Hess, 1961: 293; Rosen, 1991: 129.

[184] Cf. Hess, 1961: 137. In the mid-1840s, the notion of humanism was experiencing a conceptual boom in Hess. Cf. also Mönke, 1964: 55–6 passim.

In 1848 Marx and Engels rejected humanism, but not only as a concept with idealistic overtones. In their repudiation, they had effectively acknowledged that the term denoted a historical movement that spanned the Reformation and the Enlightenment, and that it continued through Ruge to the present. The historiographical connotation of humanism, introduced by Hagen, had persisted despite this, precisely because Marx and Engels rejected it. At the same time, Marx's 1844 assertion that humanism, communism, and atheism were all related was abandoned. In contrast, bringing up Reuchlin and Herder underlined the connection between humanism and classical languages and religion as well as, more crucially, the idea that humanism was just a religious movement, which, for Marx and Engels, ultimately included idealism.

As far as we know at present, this was sustainable. For a long time after 1848, the concept of humanism vanished from the socialist-communist literature as a quasi-"hostile" concept that had been appropriated. It bore positive connotations when it re-emerged in the Popular Front movement of the 1930s[185] before the GDR adopted it as part of its dazzling vocabulary of the "church struggle" – that is, opposed to Christian humanism – or as a compromise term to make a hegemonic claim to a common denominator between Marxists and Christians.[186]

2.8 Humanism as Lodge, Religion, and the Invisible Church: Ruge

Humanism lost its appeal for Marxist authors in the 19th century, both conceptually and in terms of content, although it was later restored in the GDR. But the path taken since humanism was linked to education, historiography, philosophy, theology, and therefore to cultural history. For that reason, it cannot ignore either Karl Hagen or Arnold Ruge, another Young Hegelian who, like Hagen, was sent as a representative of the radical democratic left to serve as a deputy in the Frankfurt National Assembly, and as an envoy from Breslau. Since 1826, he had been held captive in a fortress, and in the 1840s, he went into exile for an extended period of time. Ruge, a qualified lecturer in philosophy, had also studied under Schleiermacher, whose imprint is unmistakable in his writings. Ruge taught at

---

[185] Cf. Rüegg, 1959: 480.

[186] Hartmut von Hentig reports on a humanism conference in Wittenberg in 1961, at which humanism was "not defined, even once, and the humanism of the young Marx" was not mentioned by the GDR scholars present, although it was SED's official term paralleling socialism. Of all people, it was a West German who pointed to the currency of humanism in Marx, cf. Hentig, 1961: 85. This is remarkable in view of the fact that the concept of humanism was experiencing a boom in the state and party leadership of the GDR since October 1960. On 4 October 1960, Walter Ulbricht claimed in a programmatic declaration: "Christianity and the humanistic goals of socialism are not opposites." Cf. Marxisten und Christen wirken gemeinsam für Frieden und Humanismus, 1964, 85–6. On that connections cf. in detail now Blume, 2021.

the *Pedagogium* of the Francke Foundations in Halle, maintained an extensive correspondence with Feuerbach and was an editor in Paris with Marx. He collaborated with Bruno Bauer and David Friedrich Strauss to publish *Hallische Jahrbücher für deutsche Wissenschaft und Kunst* (Halle Yearbooks for German Science and Art) in Halle and, when they were banned, in Dresden.[187]

Ruge gave humanism a fresh critical impetus, opening up new fronts. Between 1838 and 1841, "humanism" was not a conspicuous presence in the *Hallische Jahrbücher*.[188] It does not appear in the yearbooks, in Ruge's own extensive texts.[189] It is possible that Ruge came across Karl Hagen's concept of humanism between 1841 and 1844 and during his reading in the *Vormärz* circles. As early as 1846, after the Prussian censorship court outlawed a related article, Ruge used humanism to justify the connection he had formed between Feuerbach's critique of Christianity and the socialist agenda.[190]

Ruge's programmatic text from 1849, *Die Religion unserer Zeit* (The Religion of Our Time), primarily influenced by church criticism and Feuerbach's denigration of religion, was also directed against enthusiasts, fanatics, and atheists. Yet, he held to the concept of religion, which he considered the "heartbeat of the moral world,"[191] without designating religion with humanism. Like Hagen, Ruge distinguished between Protestantism and the spirit of the Reformation; he condemned "papalism" and "Lutheran dogmatics," both of which would have tainted the "idea of Christianity." On the other hand, he claimed the connection between the "religiosity of the Reformation," the "ethical socialism of the revolution," the "seriousness of the Enlightenment" and philosophy to socialism. He considered them "real additional developments of the Christian principle of humanity,"[192] which have the "God-man" at their core.[193] This "humane religion,"[194] which saw the idea of God realized in man and suspended at the same time, could be described as a consistently anthropocentric Protestantism or as a secularized Christology of incarnation, insofar as, according to Ruge, the essence of man fulfills and completes the transcendence

---

[187] On Ruge cf. an earlier work of Pohlmann, 1979, as well as Walter 1995; Baab, 2013, 38–42.
[188] Rendered differently in Baab, 2013: 39, however, without citing the exact location. Humanism was neither mentioned even in an extensive essay on the national mission of translating Italian classics nor in the review of Ranke's history of the Reformation. Cf. Hallische Jahrbücher für deutsche Wissenschaft und Kunst 3, 1840: 144 ("by ...r"); 1697–1704 (by Klüpfel), 1945–1966; Karl Stahr in Baab, 2013: vol. 4 (1841) 11–2, 14–6, 19–20, 23–4, 27–8.
[189] Cf., for instance, Ruge, 1841: 481–2, 485–7, 489–90, 493–5, 509–11, 513–5, 517–19, 521–2, 525–6.
[190] Ruge, 1846a. This was about Ruge's two-volume work: Zwei Jahre in Paris. Studien und Erinnerungen (1846b).
[191] Ruge 1849: 10.
[192] Ruge, 1849: 13–14
[193] Ruge, 1849: 55.
[194] Ruge, 1849: 65, 74.

of the idea of God. He blamed the "deism of the terrorists" for his failure to realize his vision of a "completely secularized Protestantism," a "cult of the 'theophilanthropists'" or the "goddess of reason" during the revolution.[195] Ruge observed a split between Christianity and the Enlightenment, which, in his view, was caused by the discrepancy between the essence of revealed religion and the essence of man.[196] Yet he never made the connection between that and the Renaissance. He did not distinguish between the Reformation and "humanism" but declared that Protestantism was an extension of the Christian idea of humanity, pointing to a distinction between the two.

Evidently, he experienced a deeper rupture following the German Restoration and the fall of the French Republic.[197] Underpinning his programmatic book *Die Loge des Humanismus* (The Lodge of Humanism), published in 1852, was the assumption that Europe as a whole would be subjugated by an evil empire and Asiatic despotism. To combat the situation, Ruge declared that "The Lodge of Humanism" was an "invisible church of mankind" and that it was a task of national dimensions, and Germany's mission, to come to the "rescue of all conquests of the German spirit" as the "saviour[s] of the holy fire of intellectual freedom."[198] According to Ruge, the aim of this "open conspiracy" to create a "free, invisible, indestructible community of humanity" is the 'realization of Christianity'.[199] As part of that, he saw humanism as the culmination of a three-step process (Kant, Fichte, Hegel) in which Hegelian philosophy was realized through "practical freedom": by eliminating the contradictions between the free thinking (as acknowledged by Kant) and the unfree human world until freedom was fully realized. This revolution would be experienced in the "social-democratic republic and in the free community."[200]

Ruge, however, believed that humanism and socialism are religions rather than being purely philosophical speculation because they consistently emphasize immanence. Like Schleiermacher, he saw them as "an emotional force aspiring to approach the highest being, the true being."[201] Even though Ruge denied the existence of a transcendental dimension in the highest being, Marx and the materialists nonetheless regarded him as a theologian.[202] For the more human the god of a religion is, the truer he is.[203] Christ, who is both God and

---

[195] Ruge, 1849: 71.
[196] Ruge, 1849: 69.
[197] Cf. Ruge, 1852: 3–5.
[198] Ruge, 1852: 9.
[199] Ruge, 1852: 10.
[200] Ruge, 1852: 13–19, citation 18.
[201] Ruge, 1852: 19.
[202] Cf. also Ruge's defense against Karl Heinzen, among others, as a late consequence of the so-called Zurich atheism dispute in 1845. In: Ruge 1869: 89–119.
[203] Cf. Ruge, 1852: 19.

man, is at the core of Christianity. But as soon as the essence of Christianity is properly recognized, the whole Christian heaven falls to earth. Then a new "religion, the humane one," would emerge, where there would no longer be otherworldly gods but only living humans.[204] The transcendent god would himself become this world, although not in the sense of an incarnation. Instead, he would be understood, to some extent, in terms of religious history because Ruge believed that the new religion was rooted in the interpretation of "old" Christianity and thus was a world spirit activity but not Christology.

For the first time, Ruge's humanism emerged as a viable a socio-political program. He saw it as the continuation, completion, and fulfillment of the Christian idea of humanity, with Christ the God-man, the paradigmatic human, at its core. Although Ruge's humanism was directed against the church, he did not intend to criticize Christianity as a whole. And although humanism appears to be an anti-church concept in his work, it is not part of an anti-Christian program. *Secondly*, Ruge included older pedagogical concepts of humanism, obviously following Hagen. In addition to bringing attention to the need to address the social issue, he emphasized the importance of creating humanism-based schools and academies in order to shape the "true trajectory" of man.[205] This was to be accomplished not solely through language study but also through an understanding of the "philosophy and religion of our time," a problem that humanists would have to tackle.[206] The youth had to be educated to cultivate self-determination[207] because the free spirit was "necessarily anarchic."[208] Such a disconnection of the powers of consciousness from being and the human capacity for self-determination was unimaginable for Marx and Engels. Although Ruge had intended to address the social question, he did not endorse renouncing property or family, as advocated by Marx and Engels.[209] In his *Loge* writings, in parts seemingly a response to the *Communist Manifesto*,[210] Ruge sought to unite communism with egoism by bringing work, property, and enterprise under one umbrella.[211] For him, socialism was "the idealization of

---

[204] Cf. Ruge, 1852: 25.
[205] Cf. Ruge, 1852: 30–1.
[206] Ruge, 1852: 10.
[207] Cf. Ruge: 1852: 33.
[208] Ruge, 1852: 31.
[209] Cf. Ruge, 1852: 40–5.
[210] Cf., for instance, the final passage, which seems to be directed against Marx's and Engels' opening metaphor of the "specter" haunting Europe. Ruge, made people aware of a freedom whose spirit, it is said, could not spawn slavery, a spirit that was "formerly a guest in disguise." "And whoever sheltered it was outlawed. It has now swept through Europe like a thunderstorm, it was the master of the entire atmosphere, and its lightning tamed the slave owners." Ruge, 1852: 46.
[211] Cf. Ruge, 1852: 42.

the entire world of transport"; it was associated with the democratic republic and the "religion of humanism."[212]

Ruge's humanism was, therefore, a social agenda that was distinguished by its ties to Christianity and religion. It is remarkable, however, that although referencing the spirit of antiquity and, more specifically, Greece, in a few places, he never made any mention of a purported early modern humanism. In addition, he frequently and explicitly associated humanism with the Enlightenment as a philosophy and theology-critical movement,[213] but never as a force that would have resonated with the Reformation's spirit and then stood in opposition to it.

In his *Reden über Religion ihr Entstehen und Vergehen an die Gebildeten unter ihren Verehrern* (Speeches on Religion, Its Emergence, and Decay Dedicated to the More Educated Among His Followers) of 1869, Ruge parted ways with Schleiermacher and all traditional theology under the motto: "Instead of Schleier*macher*, we would rather play the Schleier*lüfter*," a pun on the words "*maker*" of a veil and *a "lifter"* who lifts a veil.[214] He had already classified theology as mythology in his *Loge des Humanismus*,[215] and now it ranked as the highest and most extreme form of superstition.[216] But, here, too, he stayed true to his core theme, which was the humanization of religion in order to realize Christianity. Although both religions were successful in their attempts to humanize, he categorically opposed the idea of Christ and Buddha ascending to heaven, claiming that it signified a "relapse" into the anthropomorphic world of gods on Mount Olympus.[217] Ruge believed that if Christ was allegedly the father, he was only partially human.[218] He sought to distance himself from figure of God-man, notwithstanding his support for religious anthropocentrism in 1849 and 1852 as the foundation of religious anthropocentrism. He recognized the Christian tradition that had emancipated itself from priestly speculation, but its impact in the 300 years that had passed had been partial.[219] Surprisingly, this is the only sign – albeit a veiled one – of the spirit of "humanism" in the Enlightenment that has persisted since the Reformation. In his plea to unite with the French Revolution and embrace the ethical humanism of Christianity that its motto *Egalité, Fraternité* and *Liberté*[220] embodied, he

---

[212] Ruge, 1852: 45–6.
[213] Cf. Ruge, 1852: 9, 11–2, 17.
[214] Ruge, 1869: Cover page (emphasis in original).
[215] Cf. Ruge, 1852: 34.
[216] Cf. Ruge, 1869: 3.
[217] Cf. Ruge, 1869: 29.
[218] Cf. Ruge, 1869: 31.
[219] Cf. Ruge, 1869: 36.
[220] Cf. Ruge, 1869: 39.

only went so far as to claim that "humanism and the philosophy of the Greeks" were an essential component of Christianity.[221]

This makes it necessary to keep the comparison between Ruge's humanism and the humanism of the Renaissance strictly at a phenomenological level.[222] But a historical investigation cannot be informed by such a comparison. For instance, neither Erasmus nor Marsilio Ficino even remotely agreed with Ruge's claim that the thinking human being is the highest being.[223] The same can be said of his rejection of Schleiermacher's claim that religion resides and originates in the mind. Because he believed the supposed comfort of religion is merely the avoidance of reality and the creation of delusion.[224] Man's dependence on nature had inculcated the belief in a "natural god." However, Ruge argued that Schleiermacher makes the dependence on nature the "veil 'feeling of dependence' – on anything, for otherwise our romantic friend would have brought forth the nature god, which, however, he cannot use unveiled in the pulpit."[225] For that reason, Ruge no longer saw humanism as an intellectual movement and demanded that it be linked with naturalism.[226] He saw that as the purpose of religion, which would by no means be eliminated as its materialistic adversaries had once demanded. Religion would bring heaven back to earth and help people discover their true nature.[227] It was necessary to replace the "cult of the heavenly" with a "culture of the highest goods": the thinking spirit, freedom, the principle of the good. Ruge asserted succinctly that this had long been "our current religion" in response to the potential criticism that it was neither a religion nor a substitute for religious sentiment.[228]

Ruge envisioned humanism as an idealistic, socialist, and democratic – or, as he repeatedly claimed, "social-democratic"[229] – alternative to the Marxist program. He envisioned himself as the ideal candidate to fulfill the tenets of Christianity, especially in opposition to state Protestantism, whose "ministers of culture" he regarded as *"reges sacrificuli"* (kings of the sacrificial priests).[230] Ruge believed that humanism is not a spirit that has consistently opposed or challenged the

---

[221] Ruge, 1869: 50.
[222] Pohlmann undertakes a purely phenomenological comparison of this sort, however, without taking reception into consideration, under the heading "points of contact and differences between Renaissance humanism, 'new humanism' and Ruge's thinking." Cf. Pohlmann, 1979: 141–4.
[223] Cf. Ruge, 1869: 147.
[224] Cf. Ruge, 1869: 68–9, 65.
[225] Ruge, 1869: 80.
[226] Cf. Ruge, 1869: 91.
[227] Ruge, 1869: 92–4.
[228] Ruge, 1869: 100.
[229] Ruge, 1852: 19 passim.
[230] Ruge, 1869: 36.

Reformation or Christianity, which would render it tangible from a historiographical standpoint. In his understanding, humanism is the apex of a teleological world process in which religion, including the Christian religion, and especially its theophilanthropic strand, is an indispensable segment, albeit one in need of reform.

Whether and if so, how Arnold Ruge came in contact with Niethammer's concept of humanism,[231] and that of his pedagogical successors, requires further analysis. He had used the concept of humanism with considerable modifications as early as in 1842, specifically in connection with Feuerbach. Ruge's *Loge* writings address neither language and language education, nor the notion of human intelligibility, which Niethammer emphasized and associated with otherworldliness. Ruge, who lived during the height of global spiritualism, rejected the notion of an afterlife, arguing:[232] "the whole Christian heaven falls to the earth",[233] it is no longer man who is immortal, but the "noble spirit" that dwells within humanity.[234] This could be viewed as the Hegelianization and universalization of the concept of immortality. For Kant and many other Enlightenment thinkers, the *progressus infinitus* occurs *post mortem*, free from the restrictions of the mortal body.[235] According to Burckhardt, humanism had only been around since the fourteenth century and had been defeated by the sixteenth.[236] Despite how peripheral this topic may appear in Burckhardt's reconstruction of the Renaissance, humanism is historicized as a church-critical revival movement from the antiquity that flourished between the 14th and the 16th centuries and, contrary to Ruge's and others' assertions, bore *no* connection to the trends that emerged in the 19th century.

In contrast, humanism appears in the title of Georg Voigt's major historical overview. Notwithstanding all prior concepts, Voigt adapted his idea of the historical epochality of humanism to another pivotal moment. It is no longer just a movement that is critical of the church or specifically of Rome but one that is fundamentally antagonistic to Christianity. However, Voigt did not make this definite claim in the first edition, published in 1859, but only in the second edition, published in 1880.[237]

---

[231] Wolf, 2004: 552, however, does not provide any supporting evidence for Niethammer's reading. Already in 1842, Ruge had claimed that "even in our own times, the most unruly Christ has been contaminated by humanism to such an extent that we cannot avoid recognizing that." Ruge, Eine Wendung der deutschen Philosophie. In Ruge, 1847–8: vol. 10, 387–454, here 434.
[232] Cf. overall Sawicki, 2016.
[233] Cf. Ruge, 1852: 25.
[234] Cf. Ruge, 1852: 8.
[235] Cf. Stengel, 2011a: 666–73, 685–6, 689–95, 704–8, 712 = Stengel, 2023: 765–73, 787–9, 810–4, 819.
[236] Cf. Burckhardt, 2009: 254–65.
[237] Walther, 2007a: 666, purports to quote from the 1859 edition but actually refers to the second edition of 1880/1.

According to Voigt, a well-known authority on the 15th and 16th centuries,[238] humanism began as a movement critical to the church that spread throughout Europe and vacillated on issues of dissemination of faith. However, it is important to note that in the first edition (1859), humanism denoted the "revival of classical antiquity" and was not in opposition to Christianity.[239] Only in 1880 did Voigt add that the "acceptance of what is purely human in mind and spirit, as the ancient Hellenes and Romans were wont to do, of humanity, was opposed to the views of Christianity and the church."[240] No humanist had "dared to declare himself openly and principally against Christianity or the church," although humanism was "undoubtedly a natural born enemy of the church" that "undermined its foundations."[241] Voigt's humanism in 1880 was not only anti-church but also anti-Christian.[242] In 1859, the humanists had aimed to "recapitulate antiquity *and* the pinnacle of Christian-romantic life."[243] There was no hostility between them. There was no contradiction between the two in this instance; they simply needed to be summarized and reiterated. In 1880, this passage is absent. Instead, the "Christian world" had to import and "appropriate" the vanquished antiquity of the Hellenes and Greeks. To "marry" the two and change the Christian world through antiquity is the goal of the humanists in the 1880 edition.[244] Thus the hiatus of the two currents of Christianity and the classical antiquity of Greco-Roman manner is opened up for the whole history. And humanism is henceforth an independent force. Voigt initially confined himself to the historical perspective, avoiding the complex terrain of new humanisms, anti-humanisms, or pedagogical humanisms. However, the link between Humanism and Enlightenment is then completed in 1880: the humanists were the "first apostles of the Enlightenment."[245]

That is when yet another front emerged: Voigt, who was acquainted with and quoted Burckhardt, was also aware of how much he valued Pico and Ficino. While refraining from mentioning Pico, only touching on Ficino twice, Voigt

---

[238] His works applied to the Teutonic Order, Reichstag Acts, Moritz von Sachsen, Albrecht von Alcibiades, Petrarch, among others, but one of his main works should be: Enea Silvio de' Piccolomini als Papst Pius der Zweite und sein Zeitalter, Voigt, 1856–62 (total 1551 pp.).

[239] Voigt, 1859, 1880–1, 1893: 1859, 4 = 1880, vol. 1, 3.

[240] Voigt, 1859, 1880–1, 1893: 1880, vol. 1, 4. Walther 2007a: 666, mentions 1859 as the year of citation but mentions the third edition of 1893 at the end. He only quotes the "Aufnahme des Rein-Menschlichen in Geist und Gemüth" and does not mention the opposition between Christianity and church in Voigt.

[241] Voigt, 1859, 1880–1, 1893: 1881, vol. 2, 213. The section "The Humanism and the Church" is missing at the end of the 5th chapter in the 1st ed. (1859).

[242] Baab, 2013, 36–7, does not differentiate between church and Christianity.

[243] Voigt, 1859, 1880–1, 1893: 1859, 3 [author's emphasis].

[244] Voigt, 1859, 1880–1, 1893: 1880, vol. 1, 3. In 1859, 3, the term used was not "marry" but "unite."

[245] Voigt, 1859, 1880–1, 1893: 1893, vol. 2, 486 = 1881, vol. 2, 492.

ascribes to humanism anti-esoteric qualities that, in his opinion, contributed to the Enlightenment. If Petrarch had initiated a "ruthless war [...] against astrologers and alchemists, against dream interpretation and superstition in all its forms", "we," claims Voigt, "didn't know of any humanists who would ever have made a concession to that superstitious false wisdom."[246] The anti-Hermetic bias discernible in the 19th-century debates is projected on to the early modern period. In contrast to Hagen's conception, Voigt does not mention such magical and Kabbalistic philosophers as Pico, Ficino, or Agrippa von Nettesheim, or else his list of protagonists could not have been characterized as anti-superstitious.

One redefining moment is critical: in 1880, Voigt had declared that humanism was inherently antagonistic toward the church and Christianity. A link can be made connecting antiquity with the Enlightenment, albeit via humanism and without having to be identical. Finally, humanism, initially just an educational concept, now assumes the garb of a "humanistic spirit"[247] that has spanned world history, is practiced in the church and also opposed by it. Characterized as strictly anti-superstitious, this new spirit of humanism is, in effect, an Enlightenment movement that Voigt projects back to the 18th century (Enlightenment) and the 14th through 16th centuries. Consequently, although intellectuals from Wachler to Ranke had explicitly included Hermetics, magicians, Kabbalists, and "mystics," these groups are still excluded from the humanist movement. According to Voigt, humanism is – at its root – a non-Christian bearer of science, education, and progress.

Voigt's understanding of humanism was swiftly adopted by the encyclopedias, although it was complementary to and exceeded Burckhardt's concept of the "Renaissance." Along with other entries,[248] it served as a foundation for subsequent articles, including the humanism entry in the 1885 *Reallexicon der Deutschen Altertümer* (Encyclopedia of German Antiquities), where Voigt's focus on certain aspects is most evident: Accordingly, humanism is defined as a literary "movement" related to antiquity which originated in classical antiquity and is contrasted with the "Christian-ecclesiastical principle of life of the Middle Ages," whereby the "principle of life" is also that of "humanity."[249] The fundamental conflict between Christianity/the church and humanism, which Voigt emphasizes, is, however, simply attributed to the Middle Ages, and this limitation is further applied to the German humanists with the justification that humanism

---

[246] Voigt, 1859, 1880–1, 1893: 1893, vol. 2, 486 = 492.
[247] Voigt, 1859, 1880–1, 1893: 1859, 456–7; Voigt,: 1893, vol. 1, 6. This contradicts the assertion that no Hegelian world spirit wanders through history in Voigt, according to Grendler, 2006: 308.
[248] Cf. for instance Geiger, 1882.
[249] Götzinger, 1885: 435.

was an intermediate stage in the development between the ancient life principle of "*humanitas*" and the "humanitarian ideals of the 18th century"[250] – without explicitly using the term "Enlightenment." At the core lies the "rebirth of the ancient world view,"[251] which is reminiscent of the ability ascribed to spiritual beings to reincarnate – in the contemporary reincarnation discourse and in the worldview of philosophical contemporaries.[252]

3 Ways out of the Humanism Dilemma

3.1 Humanism – Not a Viable Historiographical and Heuristic Term!

The discussion on humanism did not end with Georg Voigt. Context continues to shape humanism.[253] This remains true both before and after him: Not all humanisms could be assumed to be opposed to or separate from religion, church and Christianity,[254] and references to antiquity, philosophy, language, or the immortality of the (human) soul are not always explicit and universal. Humanism remains a contested front as a notion with numerous orientations, including philology, pedagogy, (alternative) religion and anti-religion, materialism, and socio-politics, but also as a suprahistorical being or spirit that cannot be reduced to a single common denominator without ignoring historical contexts. The historical sites where these humanisms originated are ensconced between concrete fronts. But since these 19th-century debates about the so-called origins of humanism at the dawn of the early modern period and about the humanistic spirit of the Enlightenment, the references and the historical justifications have always focused on the specific location of the respective thinkers associated with these humanisms. They choose a variety of interpretations of humanism in a way that supports and solidifies their "true" "humanistic" position.

This finding raises some questions: *firstly*, whether "humanism" can be used as an "indispensable heuristic tool"[255] in the absence of a tenable concept that is uniform and reasonably defined, and *secondly*, whether it is appropriate or helpful, and not misleading, to continue using it as a heuristic-*historiographical* instrument, in the narrower sense, when it cannot be detached from the contexts within which it is situated, and any use must necessarily blend incompatible

---

[250] Götzinger, 1885: 435.
[251] Götzinger, 1885: 439. Before Burckhardt, 2009, in 1849 already E. v. Feuchtersleben speaks of reincarnation.
[252] Cf. on the debates about Alan Kardec's Buch der Geister (1857) and, for example, the early socialist Charles Fourier, briefly Sawicki, 2016: 283, 287–96.
[253] Other concepts right into the 21st century is offered by Baab, 2013.
[254] Cf. Walther, 2007a: 666.
[255] Walther, 2007a: 668.

contexts. And *thirdly*, it is undisputed that the purely heuristic use of terms also pre-structures fields of investigation, and this is unacceptable for epistemological and critical reasons.[256]

The simplest argument would be that the *humanista* of the 14th–16th centuries were, in fact, "only" language teachers, and students of the *humaniora* were not invested in an anthropological agenda as has been widely assumed since the 19th century. Finally, the claim that a certain group is unbiased or holds a contrary opinion about the church and Christianity or religion in general raises the question of precisely which author or group of authors in any given situation represents the opposing ecclesiastical-Christian-religious front in any given instance. In a phenomenologically reductive approach, it would be necessary to define the essence of the church or Christianity in parallel with that of humanism in order to distinguish between the two. It is almost impossible to avoid extrapolating contemporary boundaries onto historical arguments, in this case, early modern debates.

Is there a way out of this dilemma? The alternatives I propose will be presented in two stages: *firstly*, to satisfy the strict historical-critical requirements and, *secondly*, to facilitate a discussion on the topic of humanism in a productive manner on the philosophical-ethical level.

Florian Baab's 2013 dissertation, which is commendable and original, not least for its theoretically critical character, focuses on systematic theology. Its main objective is to conduct a critical-dialogical analysis of anthropologies of modern humanisms. Its historical summary is unique in that it avoids discussing a humanism that is supposed to have existed in the Renaissance and antiquity. From the outset, humanism is not portrayed as a suprahistorical movement since antiquity and the Renaissance. His approach of looking at the historical semantics of "humanism" as a history of counter-terms, counter-concepts, and parallel terms is successful.[257] However, despite being aware of the irreducible polyvalence of the concept of humanism, Baab begins by offering a "formal definition" and, in the end, arrives at a point that is distinct from both humanism and theism,[258] that is, an understanding of humanism enabled by a new counter-concept that prioritizes particular interpretations of humanism that, like Michael Schmidt-Salomon's "Evolutionary Humanism," reflect an overtly atheistic worldview.[259] This model creates a new front while discarding crucial insights gained through historicization.

---

[256] Using Hinduism as an example, it was shown how the conceptualization of a cultural phenomenon pre-structures the empirical phenomena to be investigated, Fitzgerald, 2000: 19; Bergunder, 2011: 14.
[257] Cf. Baab, 2013: 23–4.
[258] Cf. Baab, 2013: 25–7, 279–85.
[259] Cf. Schmidt-Salomon, 2006; Baab, 2013: 189–217 passim.

3.2 Humanism as a Concealment Concept

The discourse history of humanism in the 19th century clearly shows that it was used as a confrontational and alternative concept. To support the thesis that, beyond this, it also functions as a term of concealment or obfuscation – despite its seemingly solely heuristic-historiographical purpose – attention is directed toward the anthropology of the 15th and 16th centuries.

The majority of authors who have studied that time period see it as one of the culminating points or even the foundation of early modern humanism. In that sense, this example highlights the confusing and distorting effects of applying humanism as a concept in practice. The alternative to "humanism" that I unequivocally propose takes into account the early modern context and avoids conflating it with other conceptual contexts that emerged in the 19th and 20th centuries. In this first step, then, I am concerned with showing the opportunities that a consistent historicization opens up for illuminating the subject of humanism and the problem described here.

It has been noted that Giovanni Pico della Mirandola and Marsilio Ficino were among the leading figures of humanism. Pico della Mirandola's text on human dignity, undoubtedly the most widely known even if not the first, is cited as illustrative of the novel aspects of the early modern anthropocentric conception of man.[260] When closely examined, neither an anti-church motivation nor a disregard for Christianity in general can be found in Pico's or Ficino's writings. The discovery of Greek, Arabic, and Hebrew texts that were previously believed to be lost forever instead gave rise to a new school of Christian philosophy and theology, and their translation sparked new discussions that eventually led to the development of Christian Hermeticism and Christian Kabbalah in the 15th and 16th centuries. Both currents were strongly influenced by a rereading of Neoplatonic as well as magical literature. This current, initiated by Italian scholars, was received by a range of influential writers and thinkers, who have been labeled as humanists since the 19th century, and include John Colet, Thomas More, Erasmus of Rotterdam, Johannes Reuchlin, Agrippa of Nettesheim, Andreas Osiander, even Sebastian Franck, but also by early opponents of Luther such as Johannes Eck[261] and Hieronymus Emser. The combined receptions of Hermetic, magical, and Kabbalistic works were associated with the prominence gained by natural philosophy, alchemy, astronomy, and other nature-magical arts.[262] One can speak of a scientific

---

[260] Pico della Mirandola, 1990. Among the lesser mentioned precursors is Manetti, 1990, cf. also Trinkaus, 2012: 230–70, 578–601.
[261] See Tortoriello, 2024; Tortoriello, 2023b.
[262] For more on these connections, see Stengel, 2013c = Stengel, 2018.

revolution at the start of the early modern period, which, however, was not connected with the demise of natural philosophy.[263]

Critical to the religious side of the discourse was the fact that Florentine theologians and their successors were preoccupied with returning to the purportedly pre-biblical and Kabbalistic writings to cultivate a *prisca theologia* and a *philosophia catholica*[264] that all devout believers in God would recognize and acknowledge. This would give rise to a superreligion that was fundamentally Christian and capable of bridging all theological and philosophical divides between the Jews, Greeks, Turks, and Christians.[265] Even for Cardinal Nicholas of Cusa, the maxim "religio una in rituum varietate" already rang true.[266]

This project was associated with an anthropology that reached its most modern incarnation in Pico's *Oratio de hominis dignitate*, his preface to the 900 theses, which gained substantial notoriety through his in-depth *Apologia* of the theses although it was never discussed at a conference. If the "anthropocentrism of the humanistic conception of man" is viewed as a negative precondition for Luther's Reformation,[267] then the *Oratio* is where this conception of man is most clearly and influentially represented. But what are its origins? For they are not revealed in the preface itself but only in the details of the 900 Theses. In the cosmic anthropology and Ficino's angelic world, which derive from the celestial doctrine of Algazel, among others, and thus from an anthropocentrism compiled from Hermes Trismegistos and the Kabbalistic sources, *Adam kadmon* is the godlike primordial man and the center of the universe, endowed with freedom of will and action, an exemplar of humanity with the power to transcend the angelic heaven with multiple divisions into the divine sphere – or to exist like cattle.[268] Pico believed that man, like a chameleon, is capable of getting rid of his corporeality. According to Pico, a man is neither earthly nor heavenly, but a divine being in human form, only clothed in human flesh.[269] Pico's human is at the "center of the world," imbued with powers that exceed the faculties of the highest spirits, because these spirits were created as spiritual automata, with no capacity for growth, which is how they would remain "for all eternity."[270] Ficino also shared the belief that man's *dignitas* came from the *divinitas* of his soul. It is superior to the material world and has an inner inclination toward God, whom it pursues as the *summum bonum*. Unlike in

---

[263] Cf. the contributions in Anstey and Schuster, 2005; Stengel, 2009.
[264] Cf. Farmer, 2008: 520–1 (thesis no. 30).
[265] Cf. Stengel, 2013c: 38–42 = Stengel, 2018: 3–5.
[266] Kues, 2003: 6.
[267] Cf. Kaufmann, 2009: 123.
[268] Pico, 1990: 6–7. For more on that: Euler, 1998: 99–122, on Ficino; Pico, 1990, 259–68.
[269] Pico, 1990: 6–9.
[270] Pico, 1990: 5–7.

Plotinus, it does not come from it; rather, it is created by it, albeit directly, *ex nihilo*.[271] There is no need for any additional godlikeness (*similitudo*), given that the resemblance (*imago Dei*) of the human soul is already a supernatural gift of God. The innate orientation of the soul toward God might be seen as a gift that essentially sets humans apart from all other creatures.[272] In Ficino's *Theologia Platonica*, humans are "Dei vicarii in terra" and because their own soul is innately in the image of God, human is "Deus in terris."[273] The Pope, *vicarius Christi*, remains unnamed; neither sacraments necessary for salvation nor priests nor even the Church appear in this anthropology. Furthermore, this anthropocentrism is profoundly theological: in casting humans as having been created first in the image of God, it is the links and not the separating factors that come to the fore.

The implications of this Hermetic/Kabbalistic/Neoplatonic anthropology are enormous, especially for the role of Jesus Christ in the event of justification – not only in Pico and Ficino but also in Erasmus, and already in Cusanus. Man's predispositions in the image of God call into question the necessity of imputing the merit extraneously acquired through Christ. However, Christ is not abandoned, but his soteriological role is significantly shifted.[274] In *Enchiridion militis christiani* from 1503, nine years after Pico's premature death, Erasmus makes the following observation about Pico's *De hominis dignitate* without specifically mentioning him, despite the fact that Pico had been officially persecuted by the church: between spirit and flesh, thanks to his divine soul, he has the freedom, and he is free to change to the side of the spirit and to ascend to the heavenly or descend to the netherworld. "The spirit makes us become gods and the flesh to animals."[275] Acordingly, man is

> divine in soul, according to the body like dumb cattle. We will never outdo the animal species at the level of the body, rather, we are inferior to them it in all its gifts. But if we were to consider the soul, we are even capable of godliness, so that we may rise above the angels and become one with God.[276]

In this conception of man, there is no room for the substitutionary atonement of Christ's death. But in this instance, Christ has a distinct function. The cross is already less prominent in Cusanus' *De pace fidei*, it is no longer at the forefront. Cusanus shifts the merit of Christ to the moment of resurrection: only through his death did the resurrection become possible in the first place, but one can

---

[271] Cf. Lauster, 1998: 48–9; Neumann, 2004: 97–9.
[272] Cf. Lauster, 1998: 51–2; Neumann, 2004: 116.
[273] Ficino, Theologia Platonica XVI 6–7, as cited in Lauster, 1998: 58, as well as 62.
[274] Cf. Stengel, 2013c: 42–4, 69–71, 79–80 = Stengel, 2018: 5–6, 21–3, 27–8.
[275] Erasmus von Rotterdam, 1995a: 143.
[276] Erasmus von Rotterdam, 1995a: 109.

partake of it only *solo Christo* and *sola fide*.[277] The rebirth restores *innocentia mentis* and the *excellentia* of the soul, also restituting original *amicitia Dei*, although Christ's soteriological particularity does not reside in his murder, rather in his excessive love and virtue.[278] Ficino and his disciple Erasmus held the view that the soul ascends synergistically only *sola gratia*, that is, specifically not as a means of self-redemption.[279] But these designs do not take account of such elements as the cross, the suffering, and the substitution facilitated through a legal relationship between God and man to be healed satisfactorily, as imprinted by Anselm of Canterbury.

The term "humanism" is often used to refer to the concept of man as it is depicted by Pico, Ficino, Erasmus, Reuchlin, and other thinkers. However, that carries a risk of conceptual confusion, because, *first*, the humanism conceived in the 19th and 20th centuries was at its core distanced from or even hostile to the church, Christianity, and even religion. Yet that is clearly contradicted by the most significant figures of humanism in the early modern period – who are not familiar with the term humanism at all. *Second*, the anthropologies of Pico, Ficino, and their recipients have little connection with *studia humanitatis* as an academic designation. *Thirdly*, these authors did not simply appropriate the antiquity of the Roman and Greek classics to form a canon distinct from Lucretius, Virgil, Ovid, or Cicero. The volumes of Ficino's translations of Hermetic, magical, Neoplatonic, and demonological literature published in Strasbourg around and after 1500 make that immediately clear. Ficino's collection of twenty demonological-Hermetic essays was published for the second time in Venice in 1516 with a dedication to Leo X.[280] *Finally*, in order to create their *theologia platonica* or a *philosophia christiana*, the Florentines and their successors employed ancient, Christian, Jewish, Arabic, and other texts that were not simply

---

[277] Cf. Kues, 1989–93: vol. 2, 53–71 (XVI–XVII); vol. 3, 89–93 (XX); Kues, 2003: 13, 42–3, 48–53. On the Christology, anthropology and theology of Erasmus and Nikolaus von Kues, cf. Stengel, 2015: 49–105, from 72 passim.

[278] Cf. Lauster, 1998: 100, 115–6.

[279] Cf. Lauster, 1998: 82–4, 110–2, 121–2, 124–56 and more. For Ficino and Pico, the generalizing statements about the allegedly completely un- or anti-soteriological theories of perfectibility and the anthropocentricity of "humanism" are to be questioned. Cf., for example, Klueting, 2007: 101.

[280] Cf. the copy in the Halle University Library, which has been worked through intensively and has numerous underlinings and an ownership entry from a Magdeburg high school: *Iamblichus de mysteriis Aegyptiorum. Chaldeorum. Assyriorum. Proclus Platonicum Alcibiadem de anima, atq. daemone. Proclus de sacrificio & magia. Porphyrius de divinis atq. daemonibus. Synesis Platonicus de somnis. Psellus de daemonibus. Expositio Prisciani & Marsilii in Theophrastum de sensu, phantasia & intellectu. Alcinoi Platonici philosophi liber de doctrina Platonis. Speusippi Platonis discipuli liber de platonis definitionibus. Pythagorae philosophi aurea verba. Symbola Pithagorae philosophi. Xenocratis philosophi platonici liber de morte. Mercurii Trismegisti Pimander. Eiusdem Asclepius. Marsilii Ficini de triplici vita Lib. II. [...]*, 1516.

translated but also compiled and adapted.[281] Designating Pico, Ficino, and their readers and recipients as humanists would lend the impression that these authors had only drawn on Plato and Aristotle and other works from Graeco-Roman antiquity, and not on the Hermetic and Kabbalistic, and other somewhat clandestine literature. Akin to the aforementioned Georg Voigt,[282] who summarily excluded Pico and Ficino from the humanistic canon, claiming there were no magical humanists, other thinkers from the 19th and 20th centuries who might have considered themselves enlightened may have deemed these authors to be equally unenlightened, mystical, or full of superstitions. This is how the genealogy of the modern era is purged of sources deemed superstitious or esoteric.

The term "humanism" is misleading as a collective term at the points indicated, because writers like Pico and Ficino distinguished themselves not from Christianity per se but from a specific understanding of Christianity, namely the Augustinian understanding, which was then fervently redefined by Luther with a soteriology and anthropology that was unmistakably anti-Pelagian, satisfactorial, and imputatory.[283] The Kabbalistic/Hermetic anthropology of Pico and Ficino and their recipients was, of course, critical of the church, as the sacramental mediating role of the priest, the Pope as *vicarius Christi*, and the sacraments – indeed, the necessity for the salvation of the church as a whole – were no longer present, which had been impressively expressed at the Fourth Council of the Lateran in 1215 under Innocent III. In this regard, especially against Innocent III's work "De miseria humanae conditionis," Pico's *Oratio* had already addressed this issue, just as its most significant predecessor Giannozzo Manetti did with his "De dignitate et excellentia hominis."[284]

Grouping such writers under the rubric of "humanism" inevitably entails claiming and defending the notion of what is "properly" and "truly" Christian, while also concealing certain theological-anthropological concepts: in relation to the "other," which, in this case, is subsumed under the modern concept of humanism that is hardly definable. For instance, if one claimed that those who do not consistently follow the Augustinian-Lutheran soteriology cannot be considered Christians,[285] then *nolens volens* the presumption is that a contemporary and specific understanding of what is orthodox already existed in the early modern period, thus universalizing it. At the same time, the primary

---

[281] Cf. Kristeller, 1972. For Pico cf. mainly Farmer, 2008.
[282] Cf. note 278 above.
[283] Cf. Stengel, 2013c. For a reinterpretation of the Reformation theology and Christology front against the background of the strict rejection of the Hermetic/Kabbalistic movement within the church, cf. now Tortoriello, 2023a.
[284] See note 292 and Segni, 1990; Wili, 1953.
[285] Erasmus had already defended himself against Luther's reproach, who, conversely, claimed to be a Christian himself, cf. Erasmus von Rotterdam, 1995b: 327, as well as 138.

concern was to validate the Christian dimension and to assert one's own brand of orthodoxy – in what tradition one classified oneself: the Augustinian or the Hermetic or another kind of Christianity.

Conversely, when humanism is used as an antithesis or alternative to the Reformation or to Christianity as a whole in relation to early modern authors, the specific references, contexts, and definitions of what Christianity is supposed to be are often obscured or obfuscated. However, these debates were precisely about which form of reformation or Christianity could be considered "true," "orthodox," or legitimate. The clarification of this question did not precede these debates; rather, it was the subject of them. Such decisions should not be made retrospectively from a perspective that was formed centuries later.

3.3 Proposed Solution I: Consistent Historicization

Pico and Erasmus were never concerned with "humanism," but rather with an angelological and demonological anthropology with magical connotations. How can one align them with later "humanist" trends? This includes: Niethammer's pedagogical approach, Marxism, which brusquely rejects Pico's and Ficino's metaphysical explanations of human images and a pathos of freedom, or Ruge's modified incarnation humanism, not to mention the socialist and non-Christian humanism of the SED, Martin Heidegger's existentialist humanism,[286] or even Karl Barth's (re-theologized) humanistic concept of God's humanity.[287]

In my view, it is improper to invoke "humanism" in reference to the early modern authors – such as Pico, Ficino, Reuchlin, or Erasmus – who have been portrayed as humanists only retrospectively. In order to do justice to both – the distinctly theological emphasis and the particular way in which so-called antiquity was appropriated – that earlier context could be referred to as "Christian Hermeticism" or "Christian Kabbalah."[288] Even though these authors had actively incorporated Neoplatonic works into their texts, Christian Neoplatonism would be an overly restrictive label given the profile of the received works. Therefore, allusions to the Renaissance's Hermetic/Neoplatonic/Kabbalistic receptions would be accurate in light of the historical context. Humanism, by contrast, is ambiguous and misleading, and from an epistemological and historiographical perspective, its heuristic use presents problems that are insurmountable. On the other hand, receptions that involved hybrid appropriations and a reconstitution of Christian and Hermetic literatures through their dynamic integration into the contemporary doctrinal structures

---

[286] Heidegger, 1991 [1949].
[287] Cf. Barth, 1950; for more on that, Baab, Humanismus, 2013: 88–91.
[288] "Hermeticism" goes beyond the reception of the Corpus Hermeticum in the narrower sense; cf. my review on Alt and Wels (2010): Stengel, 2014: 243–55, here 243–47.

and debates of the philosophical theological discourse around 1500 can be accurately described as Hermetic/Neoplatonic/Kabbalistic.

I disagree with certain researchers of esotericism who advocate using the term "esotericism," instead, in part because it originated only in the 19th century, and notwithstanding its previous sporadic use, it would be imposed on authors of the early modern period. That would undoubtedly lead to the same issues as "humanism."[289] This would, for example, amplify a deviant religious and scientific current in Ficino and Pico which runs even counter to established Christianity, even though these authors clearly identified and regarded themselves as Christian.[290] They represented a theology that differed from only the anti-Pelagian Augustinian Christianity, but it was essentially Christian, with the above-mentioned shifts in soteriology and anthropology. One could even describe Erasmus as being strongly Christocentric.

From a historical perspective, it should not be determined *post res* which form of Christianity is "true," "orthodox," or "real" to be able to distinguish it from esotericism, heterodoxia, or even humanisms. What constitutes "orthodox," "true," or lawful must be debated and is not a heuristic presupposition of a historical perspective. It would be historically appropriate to stay at the respective contextual level – knowing that concepts and receptions as well as theosophical designs and alchemical practices pertaining to Kabbalah and Hermeticism often overlap among early modern authors. Yet it becomes implausible to subsume these currents under concepts that emerged in the 19th century. A clear historical perspective, on the other hand, will prevent the early modern debates from being modified to fit into specific 19th- or 20th-century paradigms. A primary function of modern historiography should be to critique models that seek to legitimize ideological positions by decontextualizing their historical sources and reinterpreting them in light of ideological presuppositions.

Finally, in this context, I would like to reiterate the cautionary statement made by Paul Oskar Kristeller, a well-known Renaissance scholar and Ficino expert, namely, that Florentine Platonism – which, in my opinion, should actually be called Hermeticism – cannot be regarded as "humanism," as a philological reception of antiquity in the sense of the pure *studia humanitatis*.[291] It is vital to

---

[289] In my view, the fact that the term "esotericism" has been used in German-speaking countries since the 18th century in connotation with Masonic and Pythagorean currents does not make it any easier to look at it beyond these concrete contexts as a suprahistorical movement since the early modern period. Cf. on that Neugebauer-Wölk, 2013: 37–72; Stengel, 2013b: 345–348; Stengel, 2011a: 724–8 = Stengel, 2023: 832–7; Bergunder, 2008.

[290] Cf. in the case of Ficino, his work *De Christiana Religione*, which was always included in later editions of his works (e.g., in Ficino, 1641: vol. 1, 1–73). Significantly, *De Christiana Religione* is followed in this complete edition by one of Ficino's main works entitled *Theologia Platonica de immortalitate animorum*, Ficino, 1641: 74–414.

[291] Cf. Kristeller, 1980: vol. 1, 58–61, see also vol. 2, 249 as well as 11–29, vol. 2, 244–64.

prevent such anthropological-theological undertakings as those of the Florentines from being supplanted by modern concepts of humanism and having their religious motivations covered up as a result. It would make more sense to go beyond Kristeller and only use the term "humanism" in contexts where it is also historically discussed, and not as an invariant heuristic or historiographical category, for "humanism" is itself a debate. A historicization of this kind would exclude humanism, whether it had anthropological or religious implications or not, and instead simply view *studia humanitatis* as a doctrinal movement at universities during the early modern period. The boundaries established in the 19th and 20th centuries cannot be used to understand the debates of the early modern period in a way that secures one's own positions historically, as it undermines competing positions with historical scope, and, most importantly, opens the door for historical-scientific claims.[292] Only those contexts where these novel anthropologies first appeared need to be mentioned: Christian Hermeticism, Christian Kabbalah, and the current Christian Neoplatonism at the beginning of the early modern period. These currents clashed with other, frequently anti-Pelagian Augustinian theologies and with power-political authorities within the church.

3.4 Proposed Solution II: Enlightenment as Criticism – also of "Humanism"!

Given the importance of the historical context, humanism is misleading and consequently unusable as a historiographical and heuristic category. Since attempts to synthesize Niethammer, Hagen, Ruge, and Voigt, humanism has represented an effort to universalize a categorial determination that developed in specific contexts that were produced with specific frontlines. Equally, it has been understood as a suprahistorical entity that was "discovered" and needed to be revived in other historical epochs, serving to demonstrate that a truth forged in history was in fact a future project. That necessarily involves supposing that one or more "spirits" or entities exist. Diametrically opposed to a historical method, this method does not require evidence proving how receptions are linked. In the end, it comes down to a liquefaction of what is historically significant into ideas, beings, and "spirits" that acquire corporeality in history and so also shape history. The historical event is also transformed into an "ideal continuity," a "teleological movement or a natural chain." The "radical uniqueness" of the historical is not described.[293] However, it can no longer be ruled out that such an approach only serves to legitimize and fix contemporary beliefs through historical means.

---

[292] Cf., for instance, the above example of the anti-Catholic concept of humanism.
[293] Foucault, 1996: 80.

Hence, history is stripped of its meaning and its capacity for critical analysis, which can only be realized through a specific kind of historicization that is grounded in consistent contextualization and opposes the development of teleological lines of progress and concepts of eternal value.

Similar to the Enlightenment, the historical context of the authors who formulated the concept of humanism in the first place affects the response to the question of what it is. An entire network that directs interests, enables, generates questions and answers, and produces these formulations is at the core and not the viewpoint of subjects. Can "Enlightenment" and "humanism" be defined as normative thoughts or teleological processes even though their definition is context-dependent, namely as processes that have the power to influence history as supra-historical entities and are endowed with the ability to structure history and develop dialectically as a spirit striving for its self-realization? There is no guarantee that such intangible (world-) intellectual developments will ultimately surpass the status of a chimera as literary productions, nor is that historically secure. However, what happens if we choose not to follow the path of an artificial product, the knowledge of which guides our normative actions? If future-oriented projects should not be our guide, then who or what do we follow? Because "humanism" has vacillated between attribution, program, and ideal ever since it was formed as a concept, such social and intellectual-historical initiatives must inevitably come into focus. It is closely related to ideology in a significant way. Humanists have not only set themselves apart from purported non- or anti-humanisms but have also incorporated them into their own self-constitution.

To reflect about the circumstances in which "humanism" was and is being constructed, it is necessary to initially turn to the historical-critical procedure. For it is a matter of avoiding the danger of renewed dogmatism as well as future projects that are supposedly guided by the "world spirit" in the Hegelian sense.

The first suggested remedy was that the concept of humanism be strictly historicized. The second solution to the conceptualization puzzle of humanism does not address the need for historicization. It concerns the conundrum that "humanism" can be exploited for ideological purposes and is frequently used to make extremely specific, normative claims about the parameters that can be used to determine what is and is not human. Historical criticism can only highlight the polyvalences of the term, which are strongly tied to the specific boundaries of each context. It will highlight the uniqueness of humanism's definitions and critique the generalizations and claims to universality that go beyond the epistemological scope of historical criticism. Above all, this has been shown by the fact that the relationship between the various humanisms and the religious or Christian elements are entirely contradictory. In the sense of Ernesto Laclau's theory of empty signifiers,[294] humanism proves to be an "empty signifier," in which there is always a trace of previous meanings with claims to validity and frontiers, which have been contested and combined with new connotations. The fixation of the signifier humanism on a certain content had and still has a normative dimension. The humanism debate in particular makes it clear that history as historiography is a function of certain ideological positions.

Can "humanism" then still be part of a normative project if it cannot escape its contextual constraints? I will begin with a few examples of how a politically and ideologically laden notion of humanism has been criticized in the current discussion. In a second step, I will explain in more detail how humanism can be both an analytic project that critically examines its own contextuality and an ethical project.

Michel Foucault, who has been labeled as both a counter-Enlightenment humanist and an anti-humanist since the 1970s, especially by German historians and philosophers who followed Jürgen Habermas,[295] has sparked discussions about the legitimacy and normativity of a hegemonic and, generally, Western concept of humanism.

Ernesto Laclau and Chantal Mouffe dispelled doubts – or perhaps more accurately, fears – that humanism would be rejected if its principles were not given an inherent status that made them suprahistorical and hence universally valid. But they assert that it is not about humanism. Their aim is to demonstrate how modern man was created and produced. To understand the discursiveness and performativity of the concept of the human being as well as the origins of identity and subject formation, in my opinion, it is important to emphasize the notion of construction or production in this context. Laclau and Mouffe claim that only through this process will it be possible to work more effectively and without delusions "in defense of humanistic values."[296]

Edward Said, in contrast, gave particular attention to the idea that humanism is a Western invention and that it would be capable of transcending humanistic criteria, which, according to him, were ultimately an invention of Western liberalism. At the same time, Said distanced himself from Foucault and asserted himself as a humanist.[297] Homi K. Bhabha did not pursue this line when explaining the relationship between racism and, in this case, bourgeois and liberal humanism.[298] As universal normatives like humanism are ultimately dangerous ruses of power that merely disguise their particularity and

---

[294] Cf. briefly Laclau, 2002.
[295] Cf. on that Maset, 2002: 12–19, and more often Biebricher, 2005; Kneer, 1996; Stengel, 2016 = Stengel, 2019.
[296] Cf. Laclau and Mouffe, 2012: 154–5.
[297] James Clifford criticizes that: Clifford, 1988: 263–4, 270.
[298] Cf. Bhabha, 2000b: 90–1; Bhabha, 2000a: 376.

provinciality under the cloak of universality, Dipesh Chakrabarty has taken up Foucault's warning against them. Yet, in the wake of the Négritude movement, he has continued to hold on to the normative of an all-encompassing humanism, specifically the humanism of the oppressed.[299]

Thomas Biebricher has strongly criticized the use of military force, arguing that it is instead a matter of emergency aid and universalized humanism. The series of arguments put forward by Jürgen Habermas in connection with the Kosovo war, that it is about the juridification of international relations, namely, that a cosmopolitan state must be established and (military) humanitarian intervention provided for emergency aid under international law, also created the problematic situation where the "presumed criminal" (read: Serbia) ultimately decided on the "legality of a police action."[300] Habermas challenged the "rigidity of the Kantian ethics of duty" and instead opted to determine whether moral laws are valid in relation to whether they are upheld so that, under certain circumstances, they can be overridden through strategic interventions.[301] This appears to be an effort to historically secure a post-socialist progressive thinking that, so to speak, also sees itself as humanitarian and permits the use of military force to enforce humanism – and not just for the purpose of self-defense under current international law (Article 51 of the UN Charter) as in the case of Russia's imperialist war of aggression against Ukraine since February 2022, which in reality began in 2014.

Only a few contexts illustrating the ways in which humanism is discussed as an ethical norm beyond the historical dimension have been brought up in the narrower sense. Nevertheless, these humanisms also defend themselves both morally and historically, primarily in reference to the Enlightenment and understandings of the principles of (Western) humanisms.

Yet what is the use of this journey through such highly heterogeneous histories underlying debates on humanism when the safeguards of political action are problematic? In response to Michel Foucault's late demand for a consistent historicization of "humanism," I would like to return to the beginning of my remarks and raise the issue of the relationship between the Enlightenment and humanism, one of the main perspectives adopted by Niethammer to define humanism, which has Schelling followed. Foucault argues that the Enlightenment and humanism are not self-contained systems that one would simply need to recreate in order to apply them as norms for action as if all one required was a "correct" understanding of a historical process to be able to "learn" from it for the future. As a concrete historical event, the

---

[299] Cf. Chakrabarty, 2008 = Chakrabarty, 2010.
[300] Cf. Biebricher, 2005: 236–43, particularly 238.
[301] Cf. Biebricher, 2005: 240.

Enlightenment is open to historical criticism. Moreover, humanism is vulnerable to historical criticism because it is embedded in concrete discourses and which, due to its elasticity, diversity, and inconsistency, cannot stand alone as an axis of reflection but instead give rise to debates.

It should therefore first be noted that "humanism" does not precede the debates, but is precisely the subject of those debates that deal with how man and humanity are and how they should be. In this sense, "humanism" is not a category against which debates are measured and with the help of which they are evaluated or sorted. The answer to the question posed at the beginning – "What is humanism?" – is therefore: "Humanism" is itself a debate and as such must be subjected to the historical-critical procedure.

Finally, humans rely on ideas about what is human that humanism describes and justifies.[302] And that runs counter to criticism and the autonomous "permanent creation of ourselves,"[303] not as self-discovery in the sense of a metaphysical project going back to the supposed origin but as "ascetic self-invention,"[304] as "indefinite work of freedom".[305] It is not a specific or even humanistic conception of man but the principle of criticism that Foucault sees in the "heart of historical consciousness"[306] of an Enlightenment approach, in Kant's philosophy.

At the root of the call to apply one's own reason while also challenging the limits of one's own existence and the prevailing norms lies an ethical claim that Foucault derives from Kant's privileging of practical reason over theoretical reason and knowledge.[307] The epistemology is linked to relevance within the framework of an ethical stance aimed at changing the present. As a point of departure, Enlightenment is both a process in which people participate and an "act of courage" – that is how Foucault interprets Kant's famous *Beantwortung der Frage: Was ist Aufklärung?* (Answer to the question: What is Hyphenation?), which he noted in his last major text.[308] This "act of courage" marks the beginning of a process in the present and aims to clarify the relationship between the public and private autonomous use of reason.[309] It is a moment, an act that the individual, in this case, the individual historian,

---

[302] Cf. Foucault, 1990: 46–7; Hemminger, 2004: 186–211; Brieler, 1998: 605–28. Foucault expressly points out the ambivalence of "humanism," citing various strands of humanism, ranging from those that are critical of religion and Christianity to those that are Christian, theocentric, anti-science, science-friendly, existentialist, personalist, Marxist, National Socialist, and Stalinist, cf. Foucault, 1990: 47.
[303] Foucault, 1990: 47.
[304] Foucault, 1990: 45.
[305] Foucault, 1990: 49.
[306] Foucault, 1990: 47. Cf. also Foucault, 1992; Butler, 2002.
[307] Cf. Hemminger, 2004: 178.
[308] Cf. Foucault, 1990: 37–8.
[309] Cf. Foucault, 1990: 39–40.

fulfills, which must then be repeated on its own terms, and does not result in a historical conclusion by defining eternally valid truths. Enlightenment is independent of political and intellectual authorities, independent of illusions, dogmatism, and heteronomy,[310] but also, to add Foucault, independent of an eternal, universal conception of man. Because such normative determinations of the *humanum* are always generated historically and contextually. This also applies to certain Christian views on what man is and how he should be.

Between an Enlightenment, which Foucault views as a critical principle, and humanism as an action-determining norm, there is "more conflict than an identity."[311] For an authority would be pre-critical, "sacred," or untouchable if it sets norms for criticism or encourages it. On the other hand, each of these situations must be subjected to the historical-critical project. Neither the Enlightenment nor humanism should be seen as extra-discursive preconditions of discourse, for that would preclude analysis. This does not mean the demand for a "posthuman" in the sense of Rosi Braidotti as the moment of overcoming the "opposition of Humanism and anti-humanism" and the "anti-humanist death of Wo/Man." For by identifying the "fundamental premises of the Enlightenment," namely the progress and perfection of mankind through a "a self-regulatory and teleological ordained use of reason" and through a "secular scientific rationality," Braidotti asserts that there is an essential and historical core of Enlightenment (and equally of reason and rationality), which must also be regarded as a humanistic norm albeit one that must be overcome.[312] She must therefore assume a somewhat monolithic Enlightenment event, which contradicts the findings of a movement that was by no means self-contained, but on the contrary extremely heterogeneous, which was incidentally confined to certain scholarly circles in Western and Central Europe, but has since laid claim to universal validity. The genealogical findings of the present study on "humanism" also contradict this. When Braidotti assumes that "the structural others of the modern humanistic subject re-emerge with a vengeance in postmodernity,"[313] the exclusion of these "others," for example religion, is also presupposed. This finding is also contradicted by the genealogy of the "humanism" debate since Niethammer, as well as the polyvalence of the "humanism" movement, which has been limited to some parts of Europe in recent years. Instead of exclusions, we should rather

---

[310] Cf. Foucault, 1990: 41.
[311] Foucault, 1990: 47.
[312] Braidotti, 2013: 37. Cf. Braidotti, 2013: 13, where Braidotti formulates a completely essentialist concept of humanism: "Faith in the unique, self-regulating and intrinsically moral powers of human reason forms an integral part of this high-humanistic creed, which was essentially predicated on eighteenth- and nineteenth-century renditions of classical Antiquity and Italian Renaissance ideals."
[313] Braidotti, 2013: 37.

speak of marginalizations, trivializations and, above all, of subsequent ideological transformations, especially in the 20th century, which equated the historical "Enlightenment" with secularism, materialism, or even atheism.

In contrast, Foucault insists on a twofold understanding of Enlightenment. From a historical perspective, the Enlightenment is the subject of historical criticism as a phenomenon. At the same time, however, the Enlightenment also interrogates the historicization of the human existence, including its own, for which it carves out its rules.

With that, the Enlightenment, understood as Kantian philosophy and as a Kantian concept of the "exit," straddles the boundary between history and philosophy for the first time to alter the present through epistemological criticism – rather than through totalitarian projects.[314] Criticism is the "handbook" of reason that came of age in the Enlightenment, and the Enlightenment is the "age of criticism." Foucault recognizes the intersections between "critical reflection" and reflection about history in the strict renunciation of any teleology and of the question of the origin, and in its turning to actuality;[315] through this reflection, the Kantian critique of the limits of human knowledge gains historicity. And the *humanum*, as something historical, is itself exposed to a historical-critical reflection. At the same time, this critique posits decisive power in human action. Initiating that is not a logical consequence, a matter of course, or a necessity. It is ethos, an "act of courage."

In connection with Foucault and Kant, Judith Butler reiterated the critique of humanisms as normatives that limit action and produce heteronomy in some areas. She has emphasized that the critique Foucault postulates is, first and foremost, simultaneously an ethos and an attitude,[316] as Foucault himself describes it: a philosophical ethos that is nothing other than the "permanent critique of our historical being," which is not divided into a theory, doctrine, or simply a corpus of knowledge.[317] If humanism resists classification as a legitimate historiographical category for consolidating contemporary positions – that is, if it constitutes not a determinate phenomenon but rather a multi-stratified discursive arena – then the following theoretical propositions merit consideration:

1. Drawing upon Ernesto Laclau's political theory, we propose that humanism functions as an empty signifier – a discursive site wherein political negotiations unfold both within academic debates and populist mobilizations. Empty signifiers constitute contested terrains where the semantic filling of the signifier becomes simultaneously claimed and disputed. The signifier "humanism"

---

[314] Cf. Foucault, 1990: 49–50.
[315] Foucault, 1990: 41 [removed the emphasis].
[316] Cf. Butler, 2011: 38–9, 41; Butler, 2002.
[317] Foucault, 1990: 45, 53.

undergoes perpetual processes of semantic saturation while its particular content remains subject to ongoing contestation.

The impossibility of achieving universally accepted semantic closure reflects not a theoretical inadequacy but rather the inherent political nature of the signifier itself. Any ostensibly definitive filling could only be secured through what might be termed a "violent closure" – a suppression of alternative semantic possibilities that forecloses the very polyvalence constitutive of democratic discourse. No transcendent arbitrator or referee exists who might adjudicate between competing definitions in the face of this fundamental semantic multiplicity.

2. In this theoretical framework, humanism constitutes a discourse whose epistemic coordinates and foundational assumptions become the object of critical interrogation centered upon a fundamental question: What constitutes the human and humanity, and how ought these categories be configured? This inquiry necessitates sustained analytical attention to the complex articulations between knowledge, power, and ethics that traverse debates concerning humanistic discourse. The powerful interconnections binding knowledge to power, and both to ethical frameworks, must remain transparent within our critical engagement with humanistic discourse. These connections do not merely influence the debate; they constitute its very possibility, shaping the parameters within which questions of human essence and human flourishing can be meaningfully posed and contested.

3. Positioning oneself within this discourse necessarily implicates questions of reflexive self-constitution and concerns what we might term our ongoing self-invention – emphatically not self-discovery – as a project of sustained critique. This process demands recognition of our own irreducible historicity alongside acknowledgment of the historical contingency of those narratives and normative frameworks constructed within discourses that order, regulate, subjugate, and domesticate contemporary experience.

The critical imperative extends beyond the historian's conventional purview. It becomes incumbent upon us to acknowledge our own *temporal embeddedness* as well as the historical contingency of narratives and norms – including those associated with humanism – which emerge from discourses that systematically order, standardize, regulate, and subjugate present conditions. Such acknowledgment constitutes neither resignation nor relativism, but rather the prerequisite for genuine critical engagement.

The historian's responsibility encompasses ensuring that critical analysis does not terminate at the historical level but extends into contemporary praxis. This involves acknowledging both our own historicity and the temporal specificity of discursive constructions – including humanistic discourse. In this sense, historicization transcends mere academic exercise to become nothing less than a critical project of freedom.

References

Alt, P. A. and V. Wels, eds. (2010). Konzepte des Hermetismus in der Literatur der Frühen Neuzeit. Göttingen: V&R Unipress.

Anstey, P. R. and J. A. Schuster, eds. (2005). The Science of Nature in the Seventeenth Century: Patterns of Change in Early Modern Natural Philosophy. Dordrecht: Springer.

Art. Amerika (1854). Herders Conversationslexicon, vol. 1, pp. 151–8.

Art. Humaniora oder Humanitatis Studia (1735). In Johann Heinrich Zedler, Großes vollständiges Universallexikon, vol. 13, pp. 1155–6.

Art. Humanistae (1735). In Johann Heinrich Zedler, Großes vollständiges Universallexikon, vol. 13, p. 1156.

Art. Humanität (1735). In Johann Heinrich Zedler, Großes vollständiges Universallexikon, vol. 13, p. 1156.

Art. Humanität (1855). Herders Conversationslexicon, vol. 3, p. 365.

Art. Reuchlin (1856). Herders Conversationslexicon, vol. 4, p. 714.

Baab, F. (2013). Was ist Humanismus? Geschichte des Begriffes, Gegenkonzepte, säkulare Humanismen heute. Regensburg: F. Pustet.

Barth, K. (1950). Humanismus. Zürich: Evangelischer Verlag.

Beccaria, C. (1764). Dei Delitti E Delle Pene. Sine loco.

Bemerkungen zu Herrn Prof. Klumpp's Schrift: Die gelehrten Schulen nach den Grundsätzen des wahren Humanismus und den Anforderungen der Zeit. Von einem Freunde der vaterländischen Schulen (1829). Tübingen: Laupp.

Bergunder, M. (2008). Was ist Esoterik? Religionswissenschaftliche Überlegungen zum Gegenstand der Esoterikforschung. In M. Neugebauer-Wölk and A. Rudolph, eds., Aufklärung und Esoterik: Rezeption – Integration – Konfrontation. Tübingen: Niemeyer, pp. 477–507.

(2014). What Is Religion? The Unexplained Subject Matter of Religious Studies. Method & Theory in the Study of Religion, 26/3, pp. 246–86 = M. Bergunder (2011). Was ist Religion? Kulturwissenschaftliche Überlegungen zum Gegenstand der Religionswissenschaft. Zeitschrift für Religionswissenschaft, 19/1–2, pp. 3–55.

(2024). Encounters of the Brahmanical Sanskrit Tradition with Persian Scholarship in the Mughal Empire Genealogical Critique and the Relevance of the Pre-colonial Past in a Global Religious History. Interdisciplinary Journal for Religion and Transformation in Contemporary Society, 10/1, pp. 1–30.

Bertrand-Pfaff, D. (2013). Martin Deutinger – Denken zwischen Kunst und Ethos: Ethisch-ästhetische Studien zu seinem Werk. Wien: LIT.

Bhabha, H. K. (2000a). "Rasse," Zeit und die Revision der Moderne. In H. K. Bhabha, Die Verortung der Kultur, with a foreword by E. Bronfen, trans. by M. Schiffmann and J. Freudl. Tübingen: Stauffenburg, pp. 353–84.

(2000b). Die Frage der Identität: Frantz Fanon und das postkoloniale Privileg. In H. K. Bhabha, Die Verortung der Kultur, with a foreword by E. Bronfen, transl. by M. Schiffmann and J. Freudl. Tübingen: Stauffenburg, pp. 59–96.

Biebricher, Th. (2005). Selbstkritik der Moderne: Foucault und Habermas im Vergleich. Frankfurt/Main: Campus.

Blume, N. (2021). Humanismus im Kalten Krieg: Behauptung, Zurückweisung und Vereinnahmung von "Humanismus" zwischen Ost und West, Kirche und Staat auf einer Tagung 1959 in Wittenberg. Kirchliche Zeitgeschichte, 34/1, pp. 128–46.

(2022). Humanismus zwischen den Fronten des Kalten Krieges: DDR, Christentum und Befreiungsbewegung in Afrika, unpublished Diploma thesis, University of Halle.

Braidotti, R. (2013). The Posthuman. Cambridge, MA: Polity Press.

Braubach, W. (1833). Das Recht der Zeit und die Pflicht des Staates in Bezug auf die wichtigste Reform in der innern Organisation der Schule. Giessen: Richter.

Brieler, U. (1998). Die Unerbittlichkeit der Historizität: Foucault als Historiker. Köln: Böhlau.

Brucker, J. J. (1731–7). Kurtze Fragen aus der philosophischen Historie, von Christi Geburt biß auf unsere Zeiten, 7 vols. Ulm: Bartholomäus.

Buck, August (1987). Humanismus: Seine europäische Entwicklung in Dokumenten und Darstellungen. Freiburg i. Br.: K. Alber.

Burckhardt, J. (2009). Die Kultur der Renaissance in Italien: Ein Versuch. Frankfurt/Main: Fischer (= 2nd ed., 1869).

Butler, J. (1997). Sich mit dem Realen anlegen. In J. Butler, Körper von Gewicht: Die diskursiven Grenzen des Geschlechts, trans. K. Wördemann. Frankfurt/Main: Suhrkamp, pp. 257–303.

(2002). Was ist Kritik? Ein Essay über Foucaults Tugend. Deutsche Zeitschrift für Philosophie, 50/3, pp. 249–65.

(2011). Kritik, Dissens, Disziplinarität. Zürich: Diaphanes.

Chakrabarty, D. (2008). Humanism in an Age of Globalization. In B. Davis, T. Lindenberger and M. Wildt, eds., Alltag, Erfahrung, Eigensinn: Historisch-anthropologische Erkundungen. Frankfurt/Main: Campus, pp. 74–90 = D.

Chakrabarty, D. (2010). Humanismus in einer gobalen Welt. In D. Chakrabarty, Europa als Provinz: Perspektiven postkolonialer Geschichtsschreibung, trans. R. Cackett. Frankfurt/Main: Campus, pp. 149–68.

Clifford, J. (1988). Über Orientalismus. In J. Clifford, The Predicament of Culture: Twentieth-Century Ethnography, Literature, and Art. Cambridge, MA: Harvard University Press, pp. 255–76.

Derrida, J. (1972). Die Struktur, das Zeichen und das Spiel im Diskurs der Wissenschaften vom Menschen. In J. Derrida, Die Schrift und die Differenz, ed. P. Engelmann. Frankfurt/Main: Suhrkamp, pp. 422–442.

(1986). Semiologie und Grammatologie. Gespräch mit Julia Kristeva. In J. Derrida, Positionen, ed. P. Engelmann. Wien: Passagen, pp. 52–82.

(2001). Signatur Ereignis Kontext. In J. Derrida, Limited Inc., ed. P. Engelmann, trans. W. Rappl. Wien: Passagen, pp. 15–45.

(2004). Die différance. In Postmoderne und Dekonstruktion, ed. P. Engelmann. Stuttgart: Reclam, pp. 76–113.

Deutinger, M. (1853). Christenthum und Humanismus. Erster Artikel: Schein und Wesen der menschlichen Bildung. Historisch-politische Blätter für das katholische Deutschland, 31, pp. 133–52.

(1857). Das Princip der neuern Philosophie und die christliche Wissenschaft. Regensburg: Manz (Reprint: Frankfurt/Main: Minerva, 1967).

Diller, E. A. (1841). Erinnerungen an Gotthold Ephraim Lessing, Zögling der Landesschule zu Meissen in den Jahren 1741–1746: Ein Wort zum Schutz des Humanismus und zur Erhaltung aller Zucht und Lehre. Meissen: C. E. Klinkicht und Sohn.

Eger, C. (2025). Gute Poesie. Literatur, Kultur und Herrschaft in Dessau-Wörlitz um 1800. 2 vols. Göttingen: Wallstein.

Engel, K. C. (1787). Wir werden uns wiedersehen: Eine Unterredung nebst einer Elegie. Göttingen: Rosenbusch.

Erasmus von Rotterdam, D. (1995a). Enchiridion militis christiani: Handbüchlein eines christlichen Streiters. In D. Erasmus von Rotterdam, Ausgewählte Schriften, ed. W. Welzig, vol. 1. Darmstadt: Wissenschaftliche Buchgesellschaft, pp. 56–375.

(1995b). Hyperaspistes diatribae adversus servum arbitrium Martini Lutheri. Liber primus: Erstes Buch der Unterredung "Hyperaspistes" gegen den "unfreien Willen" Martin Luthers. In D. Erasmus von Rotterdam, Ausgewählte Schriften, ed. W. Welzig, vol. 4. Darmstadt: Wissenschaftliche Buchgesellschaft, pp. 198–675.

(1995c). Querela Pacis undique Gentium ejectae profligataeque: Die Klage des Friedens, der von allen Völkern verstoßen und vernichtet wurde. In

D. Erasmus von Rotterdam, Ausgewählte Schriften, ed. W. Welzig, vol. 5. Darmstadt: Wissenschaftliche Buchgesellschaft, pp. 360–451.

Essen, G. and C. Danz, eds. (2012). Philosophisch-theologische Streitsachen: Pantheismusstreit – Atheismusstreit – Theismusstreit. Darmstadt: Wissenschaftliche Buchgesellschaft.

Euler, W. A. (1998). "Pia philosophia" et "docta religio": Theologie und Religion bei Marsilio Ficino und Giovanni Pico della Mirandola. München: W. Fink.

Farmer, S. A. (2008). Syncretism in the West: Pico's 900 Theses (1486). The Evolution of Traditional Religious and Philosophical Systems. With Text, Translation, and Commentary, 2nd ed., Tempe, AZ: Medieval & Renaissance Texts & Studies, vol. 167.

Feuchtersleben, E. v. (1838). Zur Diätetik der Seele. Wien: Armbruster.

(1849). Über die Frage vom Humanismus und Realismus als Bildungsprincip. Sitzungsberichte der Wiener Akademie der Wissenschaften. Sitzungsbericht der philosophischen historischen Classe, 1849/3, pp. 222–44 [Reprint in E. v. Feuchtersleben (2006). Sämtliche Werke und Briefe: Kritische Ausgabe, vol. 3, ed. H. Pfeiffle and H. Heger. Wien: Verlag der Österreichischen Akademie der Wissenschaften, pp. 93–110].

Feuerbach, L. (1959–60). Sämtliche Werke, 2nd ed., Stuttgart-Bad Cannstatt: Frommann-Holzboog.

Ficino, M. (1641). Opera, [...] una cum gnomologia, 2 vols. Paris: Bechet.

Fincke, A. (2002). Freidenker – Freigeister – Freireligiöse: Kirchenkritische Organisationen in Deutschland seit 1989. Berlin: Evangelische Zentralstelle für Weltanschauungsfragen.

(2004). Woran glaubt, wer nicht glaubt? Lebens- und Weltbilder von Freidenkern, Konfessionslosen und Atheisten in Selbstaussagen. Berlin: Evangelische Zentralstelle für Weltanschauungsfragen.

Fitzgerald, T. (2000). The Ideology of Religious Studies. New York: Oxford University Press.

Foucault, M. (1990). Was ist Aufklärung? In M. Foucault, Ethos der Moderne: Foucaults Kritik der Aufklärung, ed. E. Erdmann, R. Forst and Axel Honneth. Frankfurt/Main: Campus, pp. 35–54.

(1992). Was ist Kritik? Berlin: Merve.

(1996). Nietzsche, die Genealogie, die Historie. In M. Foucault, Von der Subversion des Wissens, ed. W. Seitter. Frankfurt/Main: Fischer, pp. 69–90.

Frank, M. (1997). "Unendliche Annäherung": Die Anfänge der philosophischen Frühromantik. Frankfurt/Main: Suhrkamp.

Geiger, L. (1882). Renaissance und Humanismus in Italien und Deutschland. Berlin: G. Grote'sche Verlagsbuchhandlung.

Goethe, J. W. v. (1811–4). Aus meinem Leben: Dichtung und Wahrheit, 3 vols. Tübingen: Cotta.

Götzinger, E. (1885). Humanismus. Reallexicon der Deutschen Altertümer, 2nd ed., Leipzig: W. Urban, pp. 435–40.

Grendler, P. F. (2006). Georg Voigt: Historian of Humanism. In eds. C. S. Celenza and K. Gouwens, Humanism and Creativity in the Renaissance: Essays in Honor of R. G. Witt. Leiden: Brill, pp. 295–326.

Hagen, K. (1841–4). Deutschlands literarische und religiöse Verhältnisse im Reformationszeitalter: Mit besonderer Rücksicht auf Wilibald [sic!] Pirckheimer, 3 vols. Erlangen: Palm.

(1948). Über Nationale Erziehung: Mit besonderer Rücksicht auf das System Friedrich Fröbels [1845]. In F. Fröbel and K. Hagen, Ein Briefwechsel aus den Jahren 1844–1848, ed. E. Hoffmann. Weimar: Verlag Werden und Wirken, pp. 97–136.

Hegel, G. W. F. (1969–81). Werke in zwanzig Bänden, ed. E. Moldenhauer and K. M. Michel. Frankfurt/Main: Suhrkamp.

Heidegger, M. (1991). Über den Humanismus, 9th ed., Frankfurt/Main: Klostermann.

Hemminger, A. (2004). Kritik und Geschichte: Foucault – ein Erbe Kants? Berlin and Wien: Philo.

Hentig, H. von (1961). Humanismus und die DDR: Von der Ohnmacht des Namens. Frankfurter Hefte 16/2, pp. 81–92.

Herbart, J. F. (1824–5). Psychologie als Wissenschaft, neu gegründet auf Erfahrung, Metaphysik, und Mathematik, 2 vols. Königsberg: Unzer.

Herder, J. G. (1991). Briefe zu Beförderung der Humanität [1793–1797]. In J. G. Herder, Gesammelte Werke, ed. H. D. Irmscher, vol. 7. Frankfurt/Main: Deutscher Klassiker Verlag.

Hess, M. (1961). Über die sozialistische Bewegung in Deutschland (1844). In M. Hess, Philosophische und sozialistische Schriften 1837–1850, ed. A. Cornu and W. Mönke. Berlin (GDR): Akademie-Verlag, pp. 284–307.

Iamblichus de mysteriis Aegyptiorum. Chaldeorum. Assyriorum. Proclus Platonicum Alcibiadem de anima, atq. daemone. Proclus de sacrificio & magia. Porphyrius de divinis atq. daemonibus. Synesis Platonicus de somnis. Psellus de daemonibus. Expositio Prisciani & Marsilii in Theophrastum de sensu, phantasia & intellectu. Alcinoi Platonici philosophi liber de doctrina Platonis. Speusippi Platonis discipuli liber de platonis definitionibus. Pythagorae philosophi aurea verba. Symbola Pithagorae philosophi. Xenocratis philosophi platonici liber de morte. Mercurii Trismegisti Pimander. Eiusdem Asclepius. Marsilii Ficini de triplici vita Lib. II. [. . .] (1516), 2nd ed., Venetiis: Aldus et Socerus.

Kant, I. (1902–2022). Gesammelte Schriften, ed. Königlich Preußische Akademie der Wissenschaften, later Akademie der Wissenschaften der DDR, Berlin-Brandenburgische Akademie der Wissenschaften, 29 vols. Berlin: Reimer later De Gruyter [cit. as AA = Akademie-Ausgabe].

Kaufmann, Th. (2009). Geschichte der Reformation. Frankfurt/Main: Verlag der Weltreligionen im Insel-Verlag.

Kiesewetter, H. (2011). Karl Marx und die Menschlichkeit. Berlin: Duncker & Humblot.

Klueting, H. (2007). Das Konfessionelle Zeitalter: Europa zwischen Mittelalter und Moderne. Kirchengeschichte und Allgemeine Geschichte. Darmstadt: Primus.

Klumpp, F. W. (1829–30). Die gelehrten Schulen nach den Grundsätzen des wahren Humanismus und den Anforderungen der Zeit: Ein Versuch, 2 vols. Stuttgart: Steinkopf.

(1844). Das evangelische Missionswesen: Ein Ueberblick über seine Wirksamkeit und seine weltgeschichtliche und nationale Bedeutung, 2nd ed., Stuttgart: Cotta.

Kneer, G. (1996). Rationalisierung, Disziplinierung und Differenzierung: Zum Zusammenhang von Sozialtheorie und Zeitdiagnose bei Jürgen Habermas, Michel Foucault und Niklas Luhmann. Opladen: Westdeutscher Verlag.

Kristeller, P. O. (1972). Die Philosophie des Marsilio Ficino. Frankurt/Main: Klostermann.

(1980). Humanismus und Renaissance, ed. E. Keßler, 2 vols. München: W. Fink.

Kues, N. v. (1989–93). Cribratio Alkorani: Sichtung des Korans. Lateinisch-deutsch, ed. L. Hagemann and R. Glei, 3 vols., Hamburg: F. Meiner.

(2003). De pace fidei: Der Friede im Glauben, ed. and trans. R. Haubst, 3rd ed., Trier: Cusanus-Institut.

Laclau, E. (2002). Was haben leere Signifikanten mit Politik zu tun? In E. Laclau, Emanzipation und Differenz, transl. O. Marchart. Wien: Turia, pp. 65–78.

(2005). The "People" and the Discoursive Production of Emptiness. In E. Laclau, On Populist Reason. London: Verso, pp. 67–128.

Laclau, E. and C. Mouffe (2012). Hegemonie und radikale Demokratie: Zur Dekonstruktion des Marxismus, 4th ed., Wien: Passagen.

Lauster, J. (1998). Die Erlösungslehre Marsilio Ficinos: Theologiegeschichtliche Aspekte des Renaissanceplatonismus. Berlin: De Gruyter.

Liebing, H. (1986). Die Ausgänge des europäischen Humanismus. In H. Liebing, Humanismus – Reformation – Konfession: Beiträge zur Kirchengeschichte. Marburg: Elwert, pp. 147–62.

Lindner, G. (1971). Friedrich Immanuel Niethammer als Christ und Theologe: Seine Entwicklung vom deutschen Idealismus zum konfessionellen Luthertum, 2 vols. Nürnberg: Verein für bayerische Kirchengeschichte.

Luther, M. (1840). Werke, ed. G. Pfitzer. Frankfurt/Main: Hermann.

Manetti, G. (1990). Über die Würde und Erhabenheit des Menschen: De dignitate et excellentia hominis. Hamburg: F. Meiner.

Marx, K. and F. Engels (1956–2018). Werke, 44 vols. Berlin: Dietz [cit. as MEW = Marx-Engels-Werke].

(1975–). Gesamtausgabe. Berlin: Akademie der Wissenschaften [cit. as MEGA = Marx-Engels-Gesamtausgabe].

Marxisten und Christen wirken gemeinsam für Frieden und Humanismus (1964), ed. Staatsrat der Deutschen Demokratischen Republik. Berlin (East): Staatsverlag.

Maset, M. (2002). Diskurs, Macht und Geschichte: Foucaults Analysetechniken und die historische Forschung. Frankfurt/Main: Campus.

Mönke, W. (1964). Neue Quellen zur Hess-Forschung: Mit Auszügen aus einem Tagebuch, aus Manuskripten und Briefen aus der Korrespondenz mit Marx, Engels, Weitling, Ewerbeck u.a. Berlin: Akademie-Verlag.

Mühlpfordt, G. (1980). Karl Hagen: Ein progressiver Historiker im Vormärz über die radikale Reformation. Jahrbuch für Geschichte 21, pp. 63–101.

Neugebauer-Wölk, M. (2013). Historische Esoterikforschung, oder: Der lange Weg der Esoterik zur Moderne. In M. Neugebauer-Wölk, R. Geffarth and M. Meumann, eds., Aufklärung und Esoterik: Wege in die Moderne. Berlin: De Gruyter, pp. 37–72.

Neumann, H.-P. (2004). Natura sagax – Die geistige Natur: Zum Zusammenhang von Naturphilosophie und Mystik in der frühen Neuzeit am Beispiel Johann Arndts. Tübingen: Niemeyer.

Niethammer, F. I. (1808). Der Streit des Philanthropinismus und Humanismus in der Theorie des Erziehungs-Unterrichts unsrer Zeit. Jena: F. Frommann.

Niethammer, F. I., ed. (1817). Die Weisheit D. Martin Luthers, 2nd ed., 2 vols. Nürnberg: Lechner.

Pico della Mirandola, G. (1990). De hominis dignitate: Über die Würde des Menschen, ed. A. Buck, Hamburg: F. Meiner.

Plochmann, J. G. (1826a). Das Leben D. Martin Luthers. In Dr. Martin Luther's sämmtliche Werke, 1st vol., 1st Abtheilung, ed. J. G. Plochmann. Erlangen: C. Heyder, pp. 1–66.

(1826b). Vorrede. In Dr. Martin Luther's sämmtliche Werke. 1. vol., 1st Abtheilung, ed. J. G. Plochmann. Erlangen: C. Heyder, pp. v–xii.

Pohlmann, M. (1979). Der Humanismus im 19. Jahrhundert – Eine neue Religion? Arnold Ruges Auseinandersetzung mit dem Christentum. Frankfurt/Main : Lang.

Ranke, L. v. (1839–47). Deutsche Geschichte im Zeitalter der Reformation, 6 vols. Berlin: Duncker und Humblot.

Raumer, K. v. (1953). Erasmus von Rotterdam: Der Humanist und der Friede. In K. v Raumer, Ewiger Friede. Friedensrufe und Friedenspläne seit der Renaissance. Freiburg i.Br.: Alber, pp. 1–21.

Rocher, M. (2023). "Worthmann muss entweder am Gehör oder Verstand oder an beiden einen Fehler haben . . . ." Realitäten des Religionsunterrichts am Dessauer Philanthropin. Berliner Theologische Zeitschrift, 40, pp. 205–20.

(2025). "Mit Neuem Eifer an der Bildung Junger Leute Zu Arbeiten": Das Pädagogium Regium Halle und das Philanthropin Dessau im bildungsräumlichen Vergleich. Halle: Verlag der Franckeschen Stiftungen.

Rosen, Z. (1991). Moses Hess (1812–1875). Klassiker des Sozialismus, vol. 1, ed. W. Euchner. München: Beck, pp. 121–38.

Rüegg, W. (1959). Art. Humanismus II. Philosophisch. Religion in Geschichte und Gegenwart, 3rd ed., 3rd vol., pp. 479–82.

Ruge, A. (1841). Der protestantische Absolutismus und seine Entwicklung. Hallische Jahrbücher für deutsche Wissenschaft und Kunst, 4, pp. 481–2, 485–7, 489–90, 493–5, 509–11, 513–5, 517–9, 521–2, 525–6.

(1846a). Offene Briefe zur Verteidigung des Humanismus. Die Epigonen, 3, pp. 244–76.

(1846b). Zwei Jahre in Paris: Studien und Erinnerungen, 2 vols. Leipzig: W. Jurany.

(1847–8). Saemmtliche Werke, 2nd ed., 10 vols. Mannheim: Grohe.

(1849). Die Religion unserer Zeit. Leipzig: Vereins Buchdruckerei.

(1852). Die Loge des Humanismus. Sine loco: Verlag des Herausgebers.

(1869). Reden über Religion: ihr Entstehen und Vergehen, an die Gebildeten unter ihren Verehrern, 2nd ed., Berlin: Stuhr'sche Buch- und Kunsthandlung.

Sawicki, D. (2016). Leben mit den Toten: Geisterglauben und die Entstehung des Spiritismus in Deutschland 1770–1900, 2nd ed., Paderborn: Brill | Schöningh.

Schelling, F. W. J. v. (1809). [Review of:] Der Streit des Philanthropinismus und Humanismus in der Theorie des Erziehungsunterrichts unserer Zeit dargestellt von F.I. Niethammer. Jena 1808. In Schellings Werke, 3rd Ergänzungsband, München: Beck, pp. 457–80.

Schleiermacher, F. D. E. (1799). Über die Religion: Reden an die Gebildeten unter ihren Verächtern. Berlin: J. F. Unger.

Schmidt-Salomon, M. (2006). Manifest des evolutionären Humanismus: Plädoyer für eine zeitgemäße Leitkultur, 2nd ed., Aschaffenburg: Alibri.

Schröter, W. (1831). Christianismus, Humanismus und Rationalismus in ihrer Identität: Ideen zur Beurtheilung der Reformation Luthers und des in ihr wahrhaft Symbolischen. Leipzig: F. C. W. Vogel.

Schüler, C. F. C. (1829). Humanismus: Eine vorläufige Schrift. Natur, Thier, Mensch, Engel, Gott. Philosophisch betrachtet. Leipzig: Hartmann.

Segni, Lotario de (Pope Innocent III) (1990). Vom Elend des menschlichen Daseins, trans. C.-F. Geyer. Hildesheim: Olms.

Spitz, L. W. (1986). Art. Humanismus/Humanismusforschung. Theologische Realenzyklopädie, vol. 15, pp. 639–61.

Stengel, F. (2009). Art. Naturphilosophie 2. Vom Neuplatonismus zur Naturmystik. Enzyklopädie der Neuzeit, vol. 9, pp. 33–5.

(2011a). Aufklärung bis zum Himmel: Emanuel Swedenborg im Kontext der Theologie und Philosophie des 18. Jahrhunderts. Tübingen: Mohr Siebeck = F. Stengel

(2023). Enlightenment All the Way to Heaven: Emanuel Swedenborg in the Context of Eighteenth-Century Theology and Philosophy. West Chester, PA: Swedenborg Foundation.

(2011b). Prophetie? Wahnsinn? Betrug? Swedenborgs Visionen im Diskurs. Pietismus und Neuzeit, 37, pp. 136–62.

(2013a). Die SED und das christliche nationale Erbe. Händel-Jahrbuch, 59, pp. 351–9.

(2013b). Lebensgeister – Nervensaft: Cartesianer, Mediziner, Spiritisten. In M. Neugebauer-Wölk, R. Geffarth and M. Meumann, eds., Aufklärung und Esoterik: Wege in die Moderne. Berlin: De Gruyter, pp. 340–77.

(2013c). Reformation, Renaissance und Hermetismus: Kontexte und Schnittstellen der frühen reformatorischen Bewegung. Archiv für Reformationsgeschichte, 104, pp. 35–81 = F. Stengel (2018). Reformation, Renaissance and Hermeticism: Contexts and Interfaces of the Early Reformation Movement. Reformation & Renaissance Review 2018/2, pp. 103–33.

(2013d). Swedenborg in German Theology in the 1770's and 1780's. In K. Grandin, ed., Emanuel Swedenborg – Exploring a "World Memory." Context, Content, Contribution (Contributions to the History of the Royal Swedish Academy of Sciences, 43). Stockholm: The Royal Swedish Academy of Sciences, pp. 334–55.

(2014). Review of: P. A. Alt and Volkhard Wels, eds., Konzepte des Hermetismus in der Literatur der Frühen Neuzeit. Göttingen 2010. Pietismus und Neuzeit 40, pp. 243–55.

(2015). Reformation und Krieg. In F. Stengel and J. Ulrich, eds., Kirche und Krieg: Ambivalenzen in der Theologie. Leipzig: Evangelische Verlagsanstalt, pp. 49–105.

(2016). Discourse Theory and Enlightenment. Aries, 16, pp. 49–85 = F. Stengel (2019). Diskurstheorie und Aufklärung. Neue Zeitschrift für Systematische Theologie und Religionsphilosophie, 61/4, pp. 453–89.

Stiewe, B. (2011). Der "Dritte Humanismus": Aspekte deutscher Griechenrezeption vom George-Kreis bis zum Nationalsozialismus. Berlin: De Gruyter.

Stirner, M. (1845). Der Einzige und sein Eigenthum. Leipzig: Wigand.

Tomyuk, O. (2022). Humanismus-Verständnis und -Kritik in der Russisch-Orthodoxen Kirche: Zur Humanismus-Kritik und der daraus hervorgehenden Konstituierung eines spezifischen Humanismus-Verständnisses in Diskursbeiträgen russisch-orthodoxer Geistlicher, unpublished Master thesis, University of Halle.

(2023). Zur diskursiven Konstruktion von Humanismus in der Russisch-Orthodoxen Kirche. Kirchliche Zeitgeschichte, 36/1, pp. 138–67.

Tortoriello, G. (2023a). Scala Christus est: Reassessing the Historical Context of Martin Luther's Theology of the Cross. Tübingen: Mohr Siebeck.

(2023b). The Transformations of "Renaissance Aristotelianisms": The Case of Johannes Eck's Commentary to the Corpus Aristotelicum. Reformation and Renaissance Review, 25, pp. 63–81.

(2024). The Prisca Theologia in the Early Reformation Debates. Renaissance and Reformation / Renaissance et Réforme, 47/2, pp. 41–71.

Trinkaus, C. (2012). In Our Image and Likeness: Humanity and Divinity in Italian Humanist Thought. Notre Dame, IN: University of Notre Dame Press.

Vent, H. L. A. (1827). Vorwort. In M. Luther, Werke: In einer das Bedürfniß der Zeit berücksichtigenden Auswahl. Erster Theil, ed. H. L. A. Vent, 2nd ed., Hamburg: Perthes, pp. iii–xvi.

Voigt, G. (1856–62). Enea Silvio de' Piccolomini als Papst Pius der Zweite und sein Zeitalter, 3 vols., Berlin: Reimer.

(1859, 1880–1, 1893). Die Wiederbelebung des classischen Alterthums oder das erste Jahrhundert des Humanismus, 3 ed., 2 vols., Berlin: Reimer, 1859.

Wachler, L. (1822–4). Handbuch der Geschichte der Litteratur, 2nd ed., 4 vols., Frankfurt/Main: Hermannsche Buchhandlung.

Walter, S. (1995). Demokratisches Denken zwischen Hegel und Marx: Die politische Philosophie Arnold Ruges. Eine Studie zur Geschichte der Demokratie in Deutschland. Düsseldorf: Droste.

Walther, G. (2007a). Art. Humanismus. Enzyklopädie der Neuzeit, vol. 5, pp. 665–92.

——— (2007b). Art. Humanität. Enzyklopädie der Neuzeit, vol. 5, pp. 701–3.

——— (2009). Art. Neuhumanismus. Enzyklopädie der Neuzeit, vol. 9, 136–9.

Wenz, G. (2008a). Friedrich Immanuel Niethammer (1766–1848): Theologe, Religionsphilosoph, Schulreformer und Kirchenorganisator. München: Bayerische Akademie der Wissenschaften.

——— (2008b). Hegels Freund und Schillers Beistand: Friedrich Immanuel Niethammer (1766–1848). Göttingen: Vandenhoeck & Ruprecht 2008.

Wili, W. (1953). Innozenz III. und sein Werk "Über das Elend des menschlichen Daseins." In J. Koch, ed., Humanismus, Mystik und Kunst in der Welt des Mittelalters. Leiden: Brill, pp. 125–36.

Wolf, F. O. (2004). Art. Humanismus. Historisch-kritisches Wörterbuch des Marxismus, 6/1, pp. 548–53.

Wolgast, E. (1985). Karl Hagen in der Revolution von 1848/49: Ein Heidelberger Historiker als radikaler Demokrat und politischer Erzieher. Zeitschrift für die Geschichte des Oberrheins, N. F. 94 = 133, pp. 279–99.

Zimmermann, W. (1841–3). Allgemeine Geschichte des grossen Bauernkrieges: nach handschriftlichen und gedruckten Quellen, 3 vols., Stuttgart: Köhler [many ed., recently 11th ed., Berlin (GDR) 1989].

Žižek, S. (1989). Che Vuoi? In S. Žižek, The Sublime Object of Ideology. London: Verso, pp. 95–144.

Cambridge Elements

History of Philosophy and Theology in the West

Alexander J. B. Hampton
University of Toronto

Alexander J. B. Hampton is a professor at the University of Toronto, specialising in metaphysics, poetics, and nature. His publications include *Romanticism and the Re-Invention of Modern Religion* (Cambridge 2019), *Christian Platonism: A History* (ed.) (Cambridge, 2021), and the *Cambridge Companion to Christianity and the Environment* (ed.) (Cambridge, 2022).

Editorial Board
Shaun Blanchard, *University of Notre Dame, Australia*
Jennifer Newsome Martin, *University of Notre Dame, USA*
Sean McGrath, *Memorial University*
Willemien Otten, *University of Chicago*
Catherine Pickstock, *University of Cambridge*
Jacob H. Sherman, *California Institute of Integral Studies*
Charles Taliaferro, *St. Olaf College*

About the Series
In the history of philosophy and theology, many figures and topics are considered in isolation from each other. This series aims to complicate this binary opposition, while covering the history of this complex conversation from antiquity to the present. It reconceptualizes traditional elements of the field, generating new and productive areas of historical enquiry, and advancing creative proposals based upon the recovery of these resources.

Cambridge Elements

History of Philosophy and Theology in the West

Elements in the Series

The Metaphysics of Divine Participation
Alexander J. B. Hampton

C. S. Lewis on the Soul, God, and Christianity
Stewart Goetz

Popper, Philosophy and Faith
Anthony O'Hear

Leo XIII and the Rise of Neo-Thomism
Valfredo Maria Rossi

A Critical Genealogy of Humanism
Friedemann Stengel

A full series listing is available at: www.cambridge.org/EHPT

For EU product safety concerns, contact us at Calle de José Abascal, 56–1°,
28003 Madrid, Spain or eugpsr@cambridge.org.

www.ingramcontent.com/pod-product-compliance
Lightning Source LLC
LaVergne TN
LVHW011857060526
838200LV00054B/4377